MattLyn
503-

Brooklyn & Beyond

Brooklyn & Beyond

Richard G. Lynch

Dickcissel Press · Iowa City

Dickcissel Press
Iowa City, Iowa
Copyright © 2013 by Nancy Lynch
nancylynch1941@gmail.com
ISBN: 978-0-615-92180-8

No part of this book may be reproduced or used in any form or by any means without permission in writing from the publisher.

CONTENTS

Foreword vii
Preface | On Starting a Memoir ix

One The Neighborhood 1
Two Brian 10
Three Grandma 17
Four Smith 22
Five Joe 32
Six Camp Glen Hardie 42
Seven Brushes with Teeth 49
Eight Pocket Money 55
Nine A Short Visit Home 66
Ten Beyond the Fallout 78
Eleven Bones 90
Twelve Tan-Man 98
Thirteen Periodic Reminders 103
Fourteen Oskar 113
Fifteen Contrasts 120
Sixteen Freedom Lessons 125
Seventeen A Priceless Payment 128

Photographs 135
Looking Back 149
About the Author 231

FOREWORD

WHEN RICHARD RETIRED IN 2004, he set out to write down his memories of childhood and later life. Our family already knew him as a great storyteller, and his colleagues considered him an excellent author of scientific papers and grants. Therefore it was no surprise that the memoir, as he finished each chapter, turned out to be great reading for all of us.

As Rich continued his work, two alliances enhanced the writing experience for him. One was working with a writing coach, Mary Allen, a published author and graduate of the University of Iowa Writer's Workshop. With Mary's help, Rich loved fine-tuning the stories he had written and he was full of plans for submitting the stories for publication. At the same tome, he joined "Writing Your Life's Story," a group at the Johnson County/Iowa City Senior Center. After the meetings he loved to talk about the other members' stories and I know that many group members enjoyed listening to his.

Rich's first response upon learning of the prognosis of his terminal disease was "I guess I'll have to write faster." Sadly, the effects of chemotherapy and radiation left him with little strength to write or edit. One of his chapters, about his experiences at Bikini, was accepted for publication and he was compensated for it, but it never made it into print as far as I know.

We hope that this book will be enjoyed by our family, Richard's friends, and perhaps a greater circle. The stories of his childhood in Brooklyn, NY, are a wonderful chronicle of growing up in the big city at that time and his memories of the bomb tests at Bikini, a window into US history that hasn't been well recorded from the point of view of the enlisted participant.

Richard worked on the first seven chapters of this book with Mary Allen, and they are as they finished them. The later work is as Rich left it. I made changes for spelling and minimal punctuation, otherwise it is Rich's work. There is one long narrative that contains the thread of the memoir, from which he extracted the material for the individual chapters. That is there in entirety along with shorter pieces in various stages of development.

NANCY LYNCH
with
ALISON LYNCH
BRENDAN LYNCH
MATT LYNCH

PREFACE

On Starting a Memoir

YOU FIND THE PROSPECT ENERGIZING, challenging, probably fun to do. After 40 years as a pathologist, performing autopsies, teaching medical students, investigating disease, and writing scientific articles, you can't wait to get started. But after a few weeks of scribbling notes, typing pages then tearing them up, you begin to realize that attempting to write a first memoir might be as challenging as performing an autopsy on an elephant.

You're anxious to get started, but where do you begin? The body of material seems enormous, even more than you first imagined. Hidden inside are the experiences, memories and lessons that you want to pass on to your children and grandchildren.

But how do you gain access to all of this? You try, but encounter a wall that seems impenetrable. But you're determined. You find a way to cut through it and finally, you're inside. Memories start to trickle out.

But then how do you proceed? Do you just start probing around hoping to find some clue, or is there some standard protocol, some systematic approach to guide you as you reach into those deep cavities of memory. You decide to follow intuition. As you begin to lift pieces of memories from the past, you find some pieces connected. You lift out one and another comes with it. As you proceed to investigate, you encounter surprises, events recorded long ago, forgotten till now, but once excised, quickly recognized.

Some of what you retrieve seem curiosities, incidental findings, their importance not obvious; but you take note of them. Later they may prove valuable. Some of the them appear strange; others prove exciting discoveries, creating fresh insights and new directions.

As you examine the past, the body of information you recover continues to grow. You start to feel overwhelmed. How do you get your arms around something this large? How do you keep track of it all? How do you keep it organized? What does it all mean? Is any of it important? And to whom?

As you begin to lay pieces out on the table, you wonder if you should examine every detail now, or take a small sample while accessible, store it for future reference, scratch a note to yourself, and keep moving. You step back for a moment and realize the project's enormity. You've been working at this for what seems like forever. You think you know what the final document will look like, but you keep finding new pieces. Maybe it's time to stop, think back into your past as far as you can remember and begin there. This seems like a reasonable strategy, so that's where you begin.

My first vivid memories are from the summer of 1939, at age 5. I remember walking with my Aunt Anna through what seemed a fairyland at the 1939 World's Fair. I remember that same year being at Madison Square Garden standing in front of a cage that held Gargantua the Gorilla, the star of the Ringling Brothers Barnum and Bailey Circus. I stared in awe, too young to realize the cruelty of the scene. That summer I remember looking out on New York Harbor as my father pointed to a departing freighter and said the ship contained scrap metal headed to Japan, to be melted down and made into weapons for Japan's war in China. He said some people in America were trying to get President Roosevelt to stop these shipments.

My father had a fascination with ships, especially the large trans-Atlantic passenger liners that came to New York. He worked in an office near the top of a downtown Manhattan skyscraper and through its windows he could see ships as they moved in and out of New York Harbor. He became so familiar with them that, like an expert birder who identifies each Spring warbler by its song, my father knew each liner by the sounds of its horn.

We lived four blocks from the waterfront and the sounds from the harbor constantly played in the background. When a ship's horn sounded in the distance in the morning before he left for work, my father would excitedly announce that out on the harbor, headed for Europe moved the *Normandie*, the *Queen Mary*, the *Queen Elizabeth*, or some other famous liner.

I sometimes wonder if his fascination with ships provided vicarious adventure and imaginary escape from the grinding routine of work, the constant pressure of supporting a family and getting the household bills and rent paid each month. Grade school educated, he worked first as an office boy and messenger. With time and some evening classes in a business school he secured a job as a bookkeeper. He worked for almost 50 years in a small firm created by a family to manage the enormous wealth they had inherited from their grandfather, an original partner of John D. Rockefeller.

Besides doing spread sheets and tax documents, my father ran errands in the Wall Street financial district and throughout the city in those days before e-mail, fax and Federal Express. His eclectic assignments included delivering bon voyage champagne and flowers to friends of his employer who were sailing for Europe. This he enjoyed; it got him onboard a fancy ocean liner.

Most mornings my father left for work just as my brothers, sisters and I sat for breakfast. We would see him again late that evening when he came home from his second job as a bookkeeper in a shoe store in downtown Brooklyn. Sundays were when we got to spend time with him. Some Sunday afternoons he took us for a ride across New York Harbor on the Staten Island Ferry, to kids an adventure because of the many ships, tug boats, and barges coming and going. The round trip fare was one nickel. We passed the Statue of Liberty and Ellis Island seeing the same site that greeted my great-grandparents when they arrived from Ireland during the previous century. Sometimes we would see an aircraft carrier or some other military vessel. My father taught us how to tell where ships were from by recognizing their national flags. A book at home had the flags of every country, and with time I got to know all of them.

Some Sundays we rode the subway to midtown Manhattan and walked down 42nd Street to the piers along the Hudson River, the mooring sites of the largest trans-Atlantic passenger ships. Standing at the foot of the pier, looking up, necks cranked back to take in their enormous size, the ships seemed too big to be real.

One Sunday we went for the first time to see the *Normandie*, flagship of the French Line, and the fastest of the trans-Atlantic liners. Even before reaching the pier three huge red smokestacks could be seen on the horizon. When the entire ship came into view its enormous black hull, almost as long as the Empire State Building is tall, and much longer than the pier, jutted out into the river. Its dock lines, giant braids of hemp, thicker than two hands could enclose, dropped from openings in the bow like gigantic lariats lassoing the massive steel bollards on the pier. To a kid, it didn't seem possible that something so big could actually float.

I remember standing again at Pier 88 on a Sunday afternoon in 1942 looking at the mortally wounded *Normandie*, now a soot-stained, pathetic gray hulk lying on its side, partially submerged, still smoking, the victim of a fire accidentally started while being converted to transport troops across the Atlantic for the war raging in Europe. Weeks later the *Normandie* was towed to a marine scrap yard, its ultimate fate dissection by blow torch. My father had a lifelong dream of someday sailing on an ocean liner. A few years before he died, he realized his dream.

The idea of beginning a memoir with my earliest memories worked for me. I'll never get my arms around the elephant, but I keep finding interesting things inside.

CHAPTER 1

The Neighborhood

BROOKLYN IS A CITY OF neighborhoods and immigrants, their makeups constantly changing. I grew up in the Red Hook area of Brooklyn in the 1940s. The row houses lining the street where our family lived were built in the late 1800s as small, single family dwellings, their original occupants white, middle class and mostly of northern European ancestry. Fifty years later, when I lived there in a four story row house on Warren Street along with my mother, father, two sisters and three brothers, multiple families occupied most of the houses. In half a century the neighborhood had changed from Anglo-American to a marvelous amalgam of European, Latino, Middle Eastern and African-American families, many recently arrived in Brooklyn.

On our street we had families that were Irish, Italian, Syrian, African-American, French, Norwegian, Puerto Rican, Armenian and German. In most of the households except the Irish and African-American ones, the parents were immigrants. On nearby streets lived families from Cuba, Barbados, Spain, Lebanon, Yemen, Poland, Scotland, China and Greece.

When large families crowd into several thin-walled rooms in dwellings that abut each other, personal privacy becomes an abstraction. One family in our neighborhood had 19 children and several other families had 14 or more. Mothers in some large families continued giving birth after they were grandmothers. Early on, I intuitively believed that aunts and uncles were always older than their nieces and nephews, so the first time my friend Carlos told me the baby in the carriage he pushed was his uncle, it baffled me. It took me a long time to figure out how an infant could be a teenager's uncle.

We lived in a house where the owner, a German immigrant, along with his wife occupied the upper two floors and my parents rented the lower two floors. The ground floor sat several feet below street level. It had a kitchen in the rear and a living room facing the street. When you looked out the living room windows you only saw the shoes and ankles of people passing outside. The second floor had two bedrooms and a tiny bath. My parents slept in the front bedroom and the children slept in the rear, where a curtain separated my two older sisters from my two brothers and me. My younger brother Bill and I slept in a four-poster bed and my older brother Jim had a twin bed. A flame-shaped wooden turret sat glued on a spindle that extruded from the top of each bedpost. To the great distress of our mother, Bill and I would twist the wooden flames free, force the spindles through the corners of our blanket and create a tent. Then we would pretend we were Arabs living in a desert in Africa.

A small yard sat at the rear of the house, where, except on Sundays, my mother hung the wet laundry on clotheslines to dry. She washed laundry on a knuckle-bashing scrub board in a cast-iron tub bolted to a corner wall in the kitchen. Until we grew too large to fit into it, the tub with its hinged, white-porcelainized, metal lid was where on Saturday evenings my mother gave her boys their weekly bath. If a neighbor came to the door in the middle of my bath, my mother—I'm not sure why—would gently push my head down, lower the lid of the tub, tell me to be quiet and not move, then invite the visitor into the kitchen. I never knew whether the neighbor realized that crunched under the lid sat a kid, neck crooked and hair soaped, hoping the visit would be short and that the soapy water running down his face didn't get into his eyes.

Churches, almost as numerous as saloons, dotted the neighborhood. A short walk from our house took you past Roman Catholic, Eastern Rite Catholic, Methodist, Calvinist, Greek Orthodox, Episcopal, Evangelical, and Presbyterian churches, and a Quaker Meeting Hall. Two streets away stood a small Synagogue founded by the earliest Jewish immigrants to Brooklyn.

Our neighborhood was a bouillabaisse of languages, music, foods, dress, and aromas. Had the almighty charged a 20th-century Noah to collect odors instead of animals, Noah would have loaded the arc in our neighborhood.

Certain aromas allowed your nose to function as a wind vane. When aromas of coffee or cocoa filled the air, it meant winds coming from the southwest, passing over wharfs where ships from South America unloaded their cargo. The smell of fish told you that winds came from the northwest, the direction of the Fulton Fish Market in lower Manhattan. Salty air meant southerly winds blowing in off the Atlantic. Easterlies brought the smell of beer from the large breweries in Williamsburg. Westerly winds carried air in from New Jersey, sometimes with the rotten egg odor of sulfur from oil refineries—or even worse, the stench from pig farms.

On hot summer nights, sour-smelling steam belched through sewer covers in the street to join the noxious scent spewed from the ubiquitous ailanthus tree, the tree made famous by Betty Smith in *A Tree Grows in Brooklyn,* the tree that could grow between cracks in the sidewalk and in vacant lots where the soil consisted of pebbles, small rocks, pieces of glass and traces of organic matter.

Many peddlers used horse-drawn wagons. The dropped manure added to the repertoire of neighborhood smells and also complicated the fistball and stickball games we played in the streets. Depending on the factory or warehouse you passed, you smelled acetone, leather, paint, acid, coal, licorice or some other defining odor.

By far the most pleasant smells came from kitchens of households and ethnic restaurants, from markets, bakeries and confectioneries, and from the carts of street vendors. When the aroma of parmesan, oregano and garlic came from inside, you didn't have to read the sign out front to know it was an Italian market —your nose told you so. Inside the market, for a nickel you could get a big paper cup of Italian lemon ice or gelato. When you smelled anise and chocolate you knew you were near a German bakery, springerle cookies and fabulous chocolate layer cakes. The smell of exotic spices, and freshly baked pita told you you stood outside of a Middle Eastern market, where for a few pennies you could get a generous bag of fresh pistachios or a strip of chewy, dried apricot everyone called shoe leather.

Aromas shared the air with an amazing assortment of sounds. Trolley cars screeched and rattled as they scurried along steel tracks, their clanking bells clearing the path ahead. The roar of the subway erupted along with a gust of soot and dust through sidewalk gratings each time a train rushed through the tunnels below. We lived four blocks from the waterfront so sounds from the harbor were normal background. Each sound had a characteristic timbre that allowed an attentive ear to recognize its source. Musical, high-pitched whistles meant tugboats while gruff, moo-like blasts meant harbor ferries. Wailing sirens came from harbor fireboats on the move and deep bass sounds that resonated and repeated came from the horns of fog-bound freighters. My father could recognize each of the famous transatlantic passenger liners from the sounds of their horns. Like an expert birder who identifies spring warblers by their songs, my father would hear a horn in the distance and exclaim that the *Stockholm*, the *Queen Mary* or some other famous liner was passing through the harbor.

Walking around our neighborhood you might hear Italian opera,

Cuban mambos, Arabic music or *Danny Boy* coming through open windows, behind which 78 r.p.m. records spun on hand-cranked victrolas. A special treat was to stand outside the African M.E. Church on the corner of Atlantic Avenue and Bond Street listening to the loud singing, shouting and hand-clapping inside, spirited on by slapped tambourines and a pounding piano. When those sounds blasted through the church windows they defied kids on the sidewalk to stand still.

Some summer days an elderly Italian organ grinder came through the neighborhood cranking music while his capuchin monkey, attached to the organ by a leash, worked the crowd. With cup in hand the small monkey would scamper up to anybody who stopped, expectantly shaking the cup. Whenever it was successful, which was often, the monkey would dart back to the organ grinder who took the coin and, while continuing to crank out the tune, acknowledged the donor with a nod of the head, a smile and a *"gratsi."*

In spite of the great diversity in the neighborhood, the people who lived there, especially the older ones, tended to have parochial tastes. My father was an old-fashioned meat and potatoes Irishman, and to say that he lacked culinary curiosity would be a gross understatement. I know he went to his grave never having tasted pizza, Chinese food or Mexican food. To my Dad, ethnic food was a Nathan's hot dog. He responded to the mention of garlic or chili pepper with groans and facial distortions. In a neighborhood that was a literal melting pot, most families stuck pretty close to the dietary customs of their ancestors, a tradition that made me wish I was Italian.

From time to time a band of gypsies would arrive in the neighborhood, an event that triggered excitement among the young and gossip among the elders. Moving into a vacant store, covering the windows with brightly colored sheets of fabric, the gypsies, mostly women and young children, would stay for a few weeks or a few months, and then one day would be gone.

Peeking into their store it was not obvious where people slept because you only saw a small table, some rugs and a few chairs. At night the store's large windows became reddish-purple screens upon which the dim lights inside projected the shadows of human movements.

The gypsy women wore colorful skirts and head cloths, large earrings and a lot of makeup. Their children did not attend school. The gypsies didn't interact much with their neighbors. From time to time a sign advertising fortune-telling appeared in the window, but I never knew of anyone who ventured in to learn what their future held.

Our parents warned us to stay clear of the gypsies, even if they appeared to be friendly. Although the gypsies did not seem to be particularly well off, occasionally some gypsy men would arrive at the store in a fancy, polished, bright-colored Cadillac convertible. Whenever that happened the neighborhood gossip held that there had been a visit from a "gypsy king."

Summers in Brooklyn could reach extreme levels of heat and humidity. On particularly oppressive nights, in that era before air-conditioning, some people put mattresses on their fire escapes or rooftops, and slept outdoors. Whether it was blaring sirens from fire trucks, police cars or ambulances, booming sounds from a juke box in the corner saloon, or the shouting of drunks up the street arguing some fine point about last year's World Series, the noises of the city always seemed louder on hot, humid summer nights.

On blistering hot days, youngsters cooled off by taking a wrench and opening a "Johnny-pump", the local name for a curbside fire hydrant. They used a flat board to elevate the gushing stream so it formed a cool arching shower of water that fell in the middle of the street. The arrival of a police car periodically interrupted the Johnny-pump showers. After the police closed the pump and departed, the hydrant would be reopened. This back and forth, like a game of ping-pong between the men in blue and the kids, went on all day.

Teenage boys cooled off by skinny-dipping from barges moored to docks at the foot of Amity Street, a place in the neighborhood known as "bare-ass beach." Jumping naked from a barge for the first time was a lot easier than, once in the water, trying to get back up. That required shimmying naked up a thick, scratchy hemp dock line that you always made sure hung over the side of the barge before you jumped off. After accidentally tasting it, you learned to keep harbor water out of your mouth.

We took turns as lookouts. Spying a dock security guard approaching in the distance triggered the rapid retrieval of clothes and sneakers, getting them on, and then racing to the street. Once, while running along the dock headed for the street, the guard in hot pursuit, I felt the tip of his nightstick in my loin. Never a particularly fast runner, I amazed myself and my comrades by zipping to the front of the pack, as if my legs had been put in overdrive. We made it over the cyclone fence and ran for several blocks by which time the guard had given up the chase.

At the time none of us had enough sense to worry about contracting hepatitis or polio from swimming in water polluted by discharges that spewed from moored freighters and drained from rat-infested storm sewers. We were more concerned about getting too close to the occasional condom that floated in the water.

I've often wondered why none of us ever got sick swimming in the harbor. Maybe because without knowing it, we swam in a vaccine; but that's a crazy idea, I think we were just lucky.

From the late 1800s till about 1960 the area of Brooklyn where I grew up functioned as a melting pot. Then the developers arrived. They purchased houses on the cheap, gutted and renovated them, baptized the neighborhoods with quaint names, and sold the row houses to gentry for over a million dollars.

A few decades after that transformation took place, I returned and walked the streets of my old neighborhood. The 19th-century building where I attended grade school now housed luxury condominiums. A need for classrooms no longer existed. The neighborhood residents were young professionals without children. Had there been children they couldn't have played stickball because trees and automobiles lined both sides of every street.

Gone were the sounds and the smells from long ago. Gone were the ethnic markets, pawn shops and greasy spoons, replaced by organic food shops, espresso bars and nail salons. Where once stood Flynn's saloon—a notorious, rowdy brawling place on Court Street that my parents called *The Bloody Bucket*—now stood a boutique.

I stopped for lunch at Grimaldi's pizzeria—a landmark establishment on the waterfront under the Brooklyn Bridge. I sat at a sidewalk table and overheard two elderly gentleman at a nearby table discussing why they had moved away from Brooklyn.

"My neighborhood went to the dogs," one said. "On my block people started moving because they had to. The landlords sold their buildings to developers. And then all these yuppies began moving in. They're probably nice people, but you never know.

"Yeah," the second replied. "Where I lived a lot of the old shops closed. There used to be a great Jewish bakery on our corner, but when it left you couldn't get a good bagel in the whole neighborhood. You still can't. I went into a coffee shop over there this morning. The bagels they had were whole wheat and had blueberries and raisins in them. They've got a lot of chops calling them bagels. And then the guys in the back making them were Koreans."

"Thank God Grimaldi's is still here," the first man said. "I come back here a few times every year. They've got the best pizza in New York."

"Yeah," the second man said. "Old Man Grimaldi must have sold the recipe to the new owners. Did you notice that everyone working here is Russian?"

"Hey," the first said, "When you walk around this town you wonder if there are any Russians left in Moscow."

"Well, I tell you what broke the camel's back for me," the first man said. "I'm walking to the subway station on my way to work one morning and I see a crew working on this place, right on my corner. It used to be the neighborhood barber shop, but Nick, the old guy who cut hair there had a heart attack and moved to New Jersey. So I'm watching them work on this place every day, and wondering what it's gonna be. Then one night I'm on my way home and I see this sign in the window: *Haagen-Dazs*. I said to myself: 'That's it. I'm out of here.'"

CHAPTER 2

Brian

EVEN WITH ST. PETER'S HOSPITAL two blocks from our house, the first five of my mother's pregnancies ended where they began, in my parents' bedroom. Each baby was delivered by my maternal grandmother, an old hand at home deliveries—all 15 of her children were born at home.

When my Grandmother helped me into that second floor bedroom it was April 9, 1934, the country was in the midst of the Great Depression, and Franklin D. Roosevelt was early in his first presidential term. My parents named me after my Uncle Richard, a quiet man who as a teenager left home unannounced and spent two years traveling incommunicado with a circus. Grandma, a widow with 12 other children, one of them mentally and physically handicapped, all of them crowded into a row house with four bedrooms, one toilet and no central heat, had lots to distract a mother's anguish about a vanished son.

In 1944, at age 43, a complicated sixth pregnancy forced my mother to be hospitalized for the birth of my sister Mary. Born with severe hydrocephalus, she died several days later. After the baby died my father came home from the hospital and told us that our baby sister would have been welcome in our house, but it was God's will that she had died. I remember thinking it was strange that he said the baby would have been welcome. I wondered why a baby would ever not be welcome. Only later did I learn that when a baby was born with severe anomalies, sometimes the parents would elect to have the baby institutionalized instead of bringing it home.

My father also told us that when our mother came home she would be sad. When she returned from the hospital two days later, she was quiet and moved slowly. Instead of her usual color and expressiveness her face had a grayish pallor and her gaze was unresponsive. When your eyes met hers it seemed she didn't see you. Often, for months afterwards, I would enter our living room and find her sitting alone, motionless in a chair by the window, the room's drapes drawn and the lamps unlit. In spite of the darkness, I could see her tears and reddened eyes. If I said something, she barely responded. Seeing my mother so overwhelmed by sorrow saddened and frightened me. I remember wondering if she would always be sad. I knew that my father's mother had sat in a chair for a year, and then died after her infant girl burned to death in a kerosene stove accident. Looking back now, I realize my mother was experiencing a reactive depression. Unlike my father's mother, my mother eventually recovered. After the initial period of withdrawal, my mother began to leave the house for an hour or so every day to go to church by herself, where she lit candles, said rosaries and did novenas. At home she burned candles in front of the small religious statues she kept on the living room mantle and the dresser in her bedroom.

About a year later she became pregnant with my brother Brian. Because of complications her physician had her hospitalized for the birth. Brian was born with Down's Syndrome. In the hospital my mother's physician sketched a bleak picture for Brian's development and asked if my parents wanted to make arrangements for him to be institutionalized. My mother became furious at the suggestion and refused to ever see that doctor again.

The evening before my mother and Brian came home from the

hospital my father told us that our baby brother was a mongoloid, the term used then for individuals with Down's Syndrome. He said Brian was tiny and weak, and might not live very long. All of us had seen mongoloid children on the street and knew they looked different from other kids and were mentally retarded. But my sisters and brothers and I knew nothing about the challenges that lay ahead for my parents. We were happy because we had a baby brother to hold and wheel in a carriage. My father seemed pensive.

My parents were devout Roman Catholics who never questioned what they heard from the pulpit. They believed that the sentinel events in life had divine purpose—behavior being punished, behavior being rewarded, one's faith in God being tested. After Brian's birth, I overheard fragments of conversation that made me realize that in his anguish my father struggled with guilt, searching his past for transgressions that might explain why the Almighty had allowed Mary to be hydrocephalic and Brian to be born with Down's Syndrome. I once overheard him say that after Brian's birth my grandmother, concerned about more pregnancies, sternly told him: "You stay away from that girl," a comment that likely did little to assuage his feelings of guilt, and a somewhat ironic command considering her own reproductive record. It is likely that the only reason my grandmother stopped at fifteen was the death of her husband during her last pregnancy. In those years childbearing ran a significant risk of maternal and infant mortality—oddly, it was my grandfather who did not survive the final pregnancy.

Until she died in 1962, my mother devoted her life to nurturing Brian. Grade school educated, devoutly religious, she never abandoned hope that her prayers would lead to a miracle and Brian would be cured. She saved her pennies, dimes and quarters and when they grew to a few dollars, she would mail the money to some monastic order or a religious shrine where the money assured that the monks would mention Brian in their prayers and masses.

For his first two years, Brian lay in his crib, flaccid, quiet, passive, unable to roll over or sit up. Typical of infants with Down's Syndrome, Brian was an *easy* baby; he didn't fuss, and he slept most of the time. He rarely made a sound; I never heard him cry. He took food poorly and in spite of all my mother's efforts, he remained tiny, pallid and lethargic. Always delayed by years, when Brian did reach a developmental milestone my parents took it as a sign that up in the heavens their rosaries and novenas were being heard, that the candles they lit in the parish church were being seen.

Although he was severely handicapped compared to normal children his age, the constant attention, stimulation and love Brian received carried him well beyond the bleakness predicted at the time of his birth. By his teens he had learned the rudiments of chess from my brother Bill. When he learned to print, he began writing a daily calendar of his favorite TV programs and sporting events. He loved watching the slapstick of Jackie Gleason, the antics of Groucho Marx and his duck on *You Bet Your Life*, and the animals on *Wild Kingdom* with Marlin Perkins. He rarely missed an episode of *Howdy Doody* or *Kukla, Fran and Ollie*. He watched the TV broadcasts of the New York Yankees' and Met's baseball games and kept score inning by inning.

Brian developed an almost obsessive interest in horse racing. We had no idea how he came by this interest, since no one else in the family followed the ponies. Maybe he got started because sometimes when he watched the races on TV my father would look up from what he was reading and ask, "Which horse is favored to win this race, Brian?" Then Brian would look in the sports section of the newspaper to find the listed odds. Every evening he walked with my father to Maxi's newsstand to buy a copy of the *New York Daily News*, which listed the day's horse racing results and the entries for the next day's races. Brian would spend the rest of the evening at the kitchen table comparing the day's results to his predictions, and selecting his horses for tomorrow's races. Occasionally, Brian had a big day of winners. As he ran errands for our mother he would tell anyone who asked him how he was doing—neighbors on the street, clerks in the corner grocery store, nuns standing outside of the church—"I had a big day at the track."

It seemed that everyone in the neighborhood knew Brian. The shopkeepers, the cops on the beat, the old folks who monitored the passing world from windowsills high above the street, the mugs who held sway on the sidewalk outside of the corner tavern arguing some baseball trivia—they all knew Brian and looked out for him.

Brian spoke with almost everyone he met. My mother told him regularly not to talk to strangers, but there were no strangers to Brian. Some of the neighborhood men who regularly placed bets on horse races would see Brian on the street and ask if he had "any hunches" about a particular race. Some of them believed that the Almighty endowed mentally retarded children with special powers to compensate for their inherent limitations.

My mother had some childhood girlfriends who lived a few neighborhoods away. On pleasant days my mother would walk there with Brian for a visit. Some of her girlfriends' husbands learned about Brian's interest in horse racing; they sometimes phoned our house in the evening to ask about Brian's picks for tomorrow's races before they placed bets with a local bookie. The phone would ring, my mother would answer, and after a few moments of amiable visitation the man would get to the point and ask who Brian liked tomorrow in the sixth race at Jamaica, or in the third race at Hialeah. Intent on discouraging these calls, my mother would say that Brian had already gone to bed, or would find some other excuse. After hanging up she would fret with my father about a future knock at the front door from detectives investigating reports of a gambling operation. Sometimes the caller was lucky and Brian answered the phone. Once, Mr. Gambino, a neighbor, having won some money on a horse picked by Brian, arrived at our house wanting to split his winnings with Brian—my mother would have none of that.

As his communication and social skills developed, it became evident that Brian possessed an extraordinary memory, especially for events—particularly embarrassing ones—that involved my father. Quite regularly comments in a nearby conversation would trigger Brian's memory. He would interrupt the conversation and regale all present with the details of some matter never intended for public discussion. Somebody would mention they had been to a baseball game and Brian would say, "Chum,"—Brian always called my father Chum—"tell them about the popcorn." My father would respond, "Now why do you bring that up?" Then Brian would tell about the time he and my father were at a baseball game and my father accidentally spilled a bucket of popcorn all over the people sitting in the next row. Or someone would mention vacation and Brian would say: "Chum, what about the ladies' room when we went on vacation?" "Oh, don't bring that up," my father would reply. But Brian, not to be put off, would tell about the time they stopped at a Howard Johnson's on the way to Cape Cod and my father, not paying attention to the sign on the door, started to enter the ladies room and startled a woman inside. Brian may have gotten started doing this with my father because he saw that when my mother mentioned some embarrassing moment involving my father, it got lots of laughs from whatever relative happened to be present. I believe that Brian persisted in retelling these tales because they never failed to trigger a response of clownish indignation from my father.

A few months before Brian's eighth birthday I left for the Navy and, except for a few short periods, I never again had the daily contact with Brian that most of my family enjoyed. Brian lived to be 45 which at that time was unusually old for a person with Down's Syndrome.

Shortly after my father retired my mother developed breast cancer; she died a year later. My father told Brian that she was up in heaven and could look down and see them. Until my father died ten years later, whenever he said or did something that Brian thought would not have had my mother's approval, he would tap my father on the arm, get his attention, and then point a finger skyward, look up and say: "Chum, she's watching."

CHAPTER 3

Grandma

My mother's mom was the only grandparent I ever knew—but knew is a poor word choice—the only grandparent I ever met. My other grandparents had died before I was born. When I was nine, my mother—the oldest of Grandma's 15 children—began sending me to Grandma's after school each day to run errands and do chores. The year was 1943, World War II raged in Europe and the Far East, and at home the Great Depression had ended, but for most people times remained tough.

Grandma Henderson lived a block away in a three-story row house with two rooms on each floor. The house lacked central heat and hot water and had a single bathroom. The ground floor sat several feet below street level and contained the kitchen and a dining room with a heavy wooden table that almost filled the room. A coal-burning stove heated the kitchen whose walk-in closet served as the coal bin. A door off the kitchen opened into the back yard and a wooden shed that contained an ice box for storing perishable food. All the rooms in the house were small and had low ceilings. During the winter each bedroom contained a portable electric heater that radiated warmth from a bright orange wire coil set behind a protective screen, and each bed had a thick layer of blankets and quilts. Until my Uncles Richie, Jim, Willie, Eddie and my Aunt Jean left for military service in World War II, fourteen Hendersons shared four bedrooms and a single bath.

From my earliest memories Grandma always seemed old, frail, and tired. Each day when I arrived at her house I found her where she spent much of her time, sitting by a ground floor window gazing out, her line of vision at the level of passing shoes and ankles. Except for family, the window was her contact with the outside world. When she left her chair to let me in, she walked with a slow, rocking, side-to-side gait, one hand grasping her shawl, holding it tight around her arms and shoulders. As she unlocked the door she would greet me with a smile or a scratchy hello.

Grandma's attire seldom varied. Her black shawl covered a plain cotton dress and—except on hot summer days—when she sat by the window a navy blue afghan covered her lap and legs. A dowager's hump tilted her neck and shoulders forward making her appear shrunken and bent. Ashen, finely wrinkled skin covered her face, straight gray hair, bob cut from time to time by her youngest daughter, covered her ears and in back reached to the top of her neck, and only the glistening baby-blue irises that hid behind tired lids broke an otherwise achromatic facies. Sunken cheeks and pursed lips told of jaws without teeth. The first time I saw makeup on Grandma was at her wake.

Each day one of my aunts left a note telling me what I needed to do and left the money needed for purchases wrapped in a piece of paper, each end twisted like halves of a bow tie. I always felt that Grandma, although the embodiment of reticence, was pleased to see me. On the floor at her side lie her constant companion, a gentle, black, arthritic cocker spaniel who, like her mistress, moved about with difficulty. On some cold winter days Grandma would have a kettle of hot water on the coal stove and make tea for both of us, always adding sugar and condensed milk to each cup. Sometimes there would be a plate of cookies brought home the evening before from the local German bakery by one of my aunts. But most days after she let me in, Grandma just returned to her chair by the window and gazed out. I never saw her read a newspaper or a book, or wear eyeglasses. I never wondered if she knew how to read.

Prone to few words, Grandma offered little more than what needed to be said, and sometimes even less. As she sat by the window, her mind always seemed far-away. Maybe she thought about Mary, her second child, who as an infant fell from a high chair, suffered brain injury, and spent the next 60 years secluded at home, physically and mentally arrested, and emotionally unstable. Or maybe about Francis, her third child, who at 10 months died from an infection. Maybe the red-bordered flag with five blue stars on a white field that hung in her window stirred anguish about four sons and one daughter off at war in foreign lands. Or maybe what seemed absorption in thought just reflected exhaustion and depression from years of hardship, becoming a widow at age 40, left with 13 children, 8 of them younger than 15, and one yet unborn.

One of my chores involved getting fuel for Grandma's kitchen stove. Coal shortages during the war meant at times having to burn charcoal, if you could get it, or wood. When the market where I shopped for Grandma had charcoal they kept it out of sight, saving it for their regular customers and only selling them one bag at a time. When I couldn't buy charcoal, I took wood to Grandma's from a stockpile I kept in our cellar. I scavenged wood from the street. Crates in the curbside trash outside of markets and warehouses provided a free source of wood and discarded furniture provided another. I was always on the lookout for wood. When I found some I'd carry it home and with an axe my father kept in our cellar, I'd chop the wood into pieces that fit Grandma's stove. When she needed wood, I hauled it to her house in a wagon.

Another chore involved shoes. Nine grown, unmarried daughters lived with Grandma. About every two weeks I carried a shopping bag full of my aunts' shoes to the local cobbler shop to get them repaired. The leather bottoms of women's shoes didn't last long because of the pounding they took from flagstones, concrete and asphalt. Long-lasting synthetic materials didn't exist and the war made rubber impossible to get. The Spizzano brothers, two bachelors who had immigrated to Brooklyn from Italy, operated the cobbler shop. Pasquale, the younger brother only spoke Italian and worked repairing shoes at the bench, where he supervised two other Italian men, neither of whom spoke English. Giovanni, the older Spizzano spoke English and was the front-man of the business. Fashionably dressed in shirt and tie, cigarette in hand, he spoke with a heavily accented, gravelly voice that warmly greeted all who entered the shop. Going to Spizzano's was my favorite errand. I loved the smells of freshly cut leather, glue, shoe waxes and polish that permeated the air in the shop. On cold winter days Giovanni sometimes gave me some strong Italian coffee diluted with hot milk and served in a porcelainized, blue metal cup. I would climb up into the high seat usually reserved for men who stopped in for a quick shoeshine, and while I sipped coffee and watched the workers repair shoes, Giovanni inventoried the shoes in the shopping bag, and with a carpenter's pencil wrote some Italian words on the soles of the shoes and made out the tickets. Giovanni was highly respected amongst the neighborhood Catholics because when Eugenio Cardinal Pacelli, the Vatican attaché in Washington who later became Pope Pius XII, visited New York in 1939, he came to Brooklyn to see his childhood friend from the old country.

One Sunday morning when I was eleven I saw Grandma struggling up Court Street headed towards Saint Paul's Church. Dressed head to toe in widow's black, a daughter on each arm kept her upright as her frame tilted forward with each waddling step of her bowed legs. I had never seen Grandma outside of her house before. I was surprised when I saw her because she had been bed-ridden for weeks. She churned forward with the determination of someone on a mission. I wondered why she would be going to church. Maybe she sensed the end coming and needed to speak to someone.

    I doubted she went to confess her sins to a priest, because I couldn't imagine what she would have had to report. Besides, she was in such poor health a priest would have come to her house to hear her confession. I wondered if she went to speak, but not to a person. As an altar boy I had seen old women in church, dressed in black, kneeling alone before a statue at one of the small altars recessed in a dark corner at the back of the church. I never understood what they said because they spoke softly or in a foreign language, but their intonation made it seem they were having an emotional conversation with the statue. As they knelt before the statue talking, tears ran down their cheeks, they gestured with their hands and faces as if asking questions and pleading. From time to time they paused and silently stared at the statue, as if waiting for a response.

    I never learned what Grandma did in church that day. She died three weeks later at age 62. Most of her children inherited her tight-lipped character, so I learned little about Grandma from them. Maybe 14 brothers and sisters crowded together fostered taciturn temperaments. I never heard my Grandmother or any of her children speak about my Grandfather. After Grandma died whenever I heard her children talk about her nothing they said gave any insight into Grandma's persona. Maybe there were secrets best left untold. Grandma's phlegmatic nature gave no hints about who she was, what she thought, what she felt, or what she dreamed. I saw her almost every day during her last three years. I always felt good being around her and I knew she that she cared for me, but I never knew her.

CHAPTER 4

Smith

IT WAS AS IF HE DIDN'T HAVE a first name. Except for the rare kid who prefaced a *Mr.*, everyone called him *Smith*.

Tall, broad-shouldered, muscular and fit, a blue-eyed, ruddy-faced, graying bachelor in his late forties, Henry Clay Smith directed the Warren Street Community Center, a noisy, crowded place in the basement of a Methodist church in Brooklyn, a place where boys and girls played basketball, a place where kids hung out on cold winter days, a place that everyone—kids, parents, shopkeepers and cops on the beat, knew as *The Gym*.

"Man, that Smith is one tough momma! You hear what he did?", said Manny stopping his dribble and taking a jump shot.

"Yeah, I saw it. I was out there when it happened," I answered, rebounding the basketball. "I couldn't believe it," I said. "Those guys had chains and knives and Smith's out there in the middle of street yelling at them about George Washington."

As our team practiced, the gym buzzed with what had just happened outside. Two gangs of teenagers from nearby neighborhoods, their members swaggering, exchanging insults and milling about had congregated in the street in front of the gym, ready to settle some score. Overhearing boys in the gym talking about a gang fight brewing outside, Smith rushed out of the building into the street.

As I approached the gym headed for basketball practice, I saw the trouble brewing, and then I saw Smith. I'd never seen him angry before. Face flushing, arms flailing, he ran yelling into the middle of the crowd. I thought he had flipped.

"God damn it! What in hell do you boys think you're doing?" he shouted.

"Don't you know where you are? You're standing on sacred ground. You're standing right where soldiers in George Washington's army died fighting the British during the American Revolution. They died right here, fighting for freedom; for the freedom you have. They didn't die so you could do this gang crap. You're not going to dishonor them and desecrate this hallowed ground. Now, get the hell out of here!"

Stymied, the gang members began looking at each other, shuffling feet, fumbling, grumbling; mumbling obscenities about this crazy old man. Amazingly, their bravado faded and they began drifting away.

I'd lived on that street for 15 years and never knew that George Washington and his troops had fought there. Later I learned that Smith hadn't called the police before running out into the street, and that he didn't have a back up plan had his actions failed. As the years passed and I got to know him, I came to understand that the way he handled the incident that evening was not a ploy: he believed every word he shouted about hallowed ground.

The crowded, noisy Brooklyn streets, where horns and sirens blared day and night, trolley cars screeched and rattled, and subway trains rumbled in tunnels below the pavement, were about as different as they could get from the quiet lanes of Freeville, New York, the small rural village near Ithaca, where Smith grew up. He graduated from Cornell University with a degree in Agriculture and following discharge from the Army at the end of World War I, he took a job with the Southern Pacific Railroad in Baton Rouge, Louisiana. The railroad owned vast parcels of tillable land along their right-of-ways, acreages that were farmed by sharecroppers. The railroad hired Smith to teach tenant farmers methods to optimize crop production. For the first time in his life he came face-to-face with the effects of poverty and poor education on people's lives.

After twelve years he left Louisiana to enroll at New York University with the goal of becoming a social worker. Smith never spoke about why he left Louisiana, except for an occasional hint about run-ins with the political machine of Louisiana's infamous governor, Huey Long. Anyone who spent time around Smith soon learned that strong egalitarian principles drove his actions, and that he spoke his mind. These traits and his departure from Louisiana, I have little doubt, were closely connected.

Smith arrived in New York City in the midst of the Great Depression. He found a job as custodian of a Methodist Church in Brooklyn. In return for looking after the property, he received a small salary and rent-free space in two rooms of the adjacent parsonage. The job fit his student needs; flexible hours and a short subway ride to classes at NYU.

The tall brownstone church, a Brooklyn landmark, once hosted large, vigorous congregations. By the time Smith became its caretaker, things had changed. During the early 1900s demographics evolved and the neighborhood became populated with Irish, Italian and Lebanese Roman Catholics, and by Latinos and African-Americans belonging to evangelical Christian sects. As these populations grew, the Methodist congregation of Anglo-Americans withered, its minister left, and eventually the church closed its doors.

Soon after moving to Brooklyn, Smith realized that the area around the church acted as a magnet for kids. The street in front functioned as a neighborhood playground, a place where kids played fist ball, stickball and touch football. Across the street stood the massive four story, windowless brick wall of a furniture warehouse, the neighborhood's premier wall for handball games. In the unpaved alley between the church and parsonage kids played cards, sneaked cigarettes and lit fires to cook *Mickeys,* potatoes jammed onto the end of a stick.

With time Smith got to know some of the boys. When a group of them asked about playing in the large, heated church basement on cold winter days, a place they sometimes explored through an unlocked window, Smith recognized an opportunity. He approached the Board of the Methodist Church in New York and proposed that the basement be developed into a non-sectarian community center. The Board responded positively, and raised funds to equip the facility and convert the basement meeting hall into a basketball court.

By age 14 basketball had become my passion. One Sunday morning soon after our team began playing at the gym, the pastor of St. Paul's Catholic Church announced from the pulpit that the gym was a Protestant missionary activity aimed at converting children to become Methodists. He told parents it was their duty to prohibit their children from going to the gym.

When my parents told me I couldn't go, I countered that the gym was the best place around to play basketball and that nothing religious took place there. My parents didn't budge. To them, especially my mother, if the pastor said not to go, that settled it. My mother always seemed intimidated by priests. She held them in awe. I know that she hoped one of her boys would become one. That I ignored the pastor's order upset and worried her. To me the issue was basketball, not religion.

Before basketball I had been an altar boy at St. Paul's Church for five years. I had seen priests up close. Most of them seemed to be decent men, many were quiet and formal, a few relaxed and outgoing. The pastor, a shrimp of a man, was arrogant and a bully. Sometimes he would berate a priest or the choir director while an altar boy or the sexton stood nearby. He seemed to take pleasure in intimidating people. When he was around, the nuns who came to clean the altar gave him lots of room and went about their chores nervously, as if they worked in a mine field. Sometimes when the housekeeper was gone, one of the priests would ask me to come to the rectory and answer the door during evening visiting hours. That's when parishioners came to get a copy of a baptism certificate, arrange for a funeral, or talk to a priest about some personal problem. Young couples preparing for marriage came to be instructed by a priest about the church's rules for married life. A pleasantly plump, matronly German woman prepared the priests' meals in the biggest, fanciest kitchen I'd ever seen. Outside a two car garage stood at the end of the gated driveway. The priests, especially the pastor, lived well. Some came and went in street clothes. Until then, I didn't know that priests wore street clothes. I never told my parents about the alcohol on the pastor's breath or about the time I startled him and a lady friend coming out of his bedroom.

 I continued to go to the gym hoping the conflict would smolder then run out of gas. The parents of a few of my teammates ignored the pastor's edict. He continued to deliver warnings from the pulpit about the danger of children "losing their faith and their souls." The conflict with my parents continued. My mother discussed it with my Aunt Lillie, my father's sister. A devout, unworldly Dominican nun in her mid-forties, my Aunt frequently visited our house. Orphaned along with five brothers at age ten, she was placed by relatives in a convent of Dominican nuns in New Jersey. She stayed for life. When Aunt Lillie learned I was hanging out in a Protestant church, she had the nuns in her convent pray for me. Sometimes when she asked me if I still went to the "Protestant gym", tears would well in her eyes.

 I hoped that my father would be influenced by my teammates' parents who had ignored the pastor's order. I knew that on rare occasions my father could be critical of a pastor's action. Once as he came up the subway steps in lower Manhattan he saw two nuns out on the sidewalk, holding cups, begging for money. One of them was my Aunt Lillie. My father flipped. He ordered her to stop begging and return to the convent. My aunt began weeping and asked my father to leave. He persisted. She insisted she had to stay and obey the orders of her superior who had sent the nuns out to beg because the convent needed money to buy food. My father wouldn't give up. He told my aunt: "No sister of mine is going to beg for money on the streets while her pastor drives around in a fancy Packard." My father had seen the pastor come and go in the Packard when he visited Aunt Lillie at the convent. The commotion created by my father attracted onlookers causing my aunt and her partner to leave and return to the convent.

When my father arrived home that evening, he told my mother about finding Aunt Lillie out on the street begging for money. When he told my mother what he said about the pastor and the Packard, my mother exclaimed: "Jimmy, you will burn in hell for saying things like that!" I know she believed what she said.

I kept playing basketball at the gym and eventually my parents stopped pressing. The gym's basketball court, about 70% the size of a regulation court, had some odd features, features that gave teams a home court advantage. Its small size did not allow for sidelines or out-of-bounds space. If the ball hit a wall, it was out of bounds. On fast breaks, to avoid getting creamed after making a lay-up, you learned to rotate your body in mid-air so that you rolled off the wall using your hands and feet. The court had several dead spots, places where because of loose floor boards, the basketball didn't bounce. At another spot, the floor bulged slightly causing the ball to bounce back faster, and at an unpredictable angle. Along the base of one of the side walls, a 6-inch steam pipe ran the length of the court, creating another source of erratic bounces. Shots taken from much behind the foul line hit the low ceiling if they had much arc. Some of us mastered the straight line jump shot, a peculiarity that attracted attention when we played an away game on a court with high ceilings.

In one corner at the end of the court a door opened to a flight of concrete stairs leading down to the furnace room and coal bin. The door, almost always closed, opened once during a game. As my teammate Anthony, a bit of a portly kid, raced down the court, his eye on the basket, he left his feet and released a beautiful, over-the-head hook shot. Airborne and expecting to roll off the door, he rotated his body, but then disappeared through the opening into the furnace room as the ball cleanly swished through the net, scoring two points. The referee called time while several of us retrieved Anthony from atop the coal pile in the furnace room. Sore, cut, blackened and shaken, he sat out the rest of the game, fortunately with all bones intact.

Not everything at the gym revolved around basketball. Smith saw talent and potential in everyone, and had a knack for making each kid feel special. The youngsters who came to the gym exhibited a diverse spectrum of abilities, attitudes, interests and behaviors. Many came to play basketball. Others just wanted a place to hang out. Some were tough mugs, a few were sociopaths; most were just regular kids. When some kids showed an interest in woodworking or another craft, Smith would arrange for a neighborhood artisan to come to the gym and teach some classes. When Smith saw a kid interested in music, he always found ways to promote it. From time to time he would take a group of boys interested in music to a Saturday afternoon performance at the old Metropolitan Opera House in Manhattan. They would sit in the upper balcony, up with the aficionados, up where people with standing room tickets sometimes came with a small table and sat behind the wall of the last row playing chess, listening to the opera, but not watching it.

Smith never missed a chance to talk about the responsibilities of individuals, be they citizens living in a free society, or kids hanging out on a street corner. The constant bedlam in the gym, doors slamming as kids came and went; feet and basketballs pounding the wooden floor boards, the din of kids yelling and laughing, none of this seemed to interfere with Smith overseeing the goings on from his perch on the balcony railing while talking with some youngsters about subjects ranging from baseball to botany to ethical principles.

Once he took a bunch of us to see a Broadway performance of Arthur Miller's adaptation of Ibsen's "An Enemy of the People", a play about a doctor in a small Norwegian village who discovers that the waters of the spa, the village's cash cow, are contaminated and endangering the health of the tourists. The doctor suffers the wrath of the entire community when he, alone in his opinion, urges that the spa be closed. None of us had ever been to Broadway before, no less seen a live play with professional actors. We sat in the balcony of the small theatre, some of us wearing our Sunday best, others wearing their team jacket and sneakers. I don't remember anyone looking at us, but some must have wondered about this handsome silver-haired gentleman and the mixed salad contingent of kids sitting on both sides of him.

On the subway ride home we couldn't stop talking about the play, especially how real everything seemed. When the theatre lights darkened the action on the stage made you feel you were in that small town in Norway. We were all amazed at the acting. I wondered, "How could people remember all their lines and movements, and do everything so convincingly?" For weeks afterwards we talked about the play and what it meant.

Looking back, basketball changed my life. Had I not played basketball, I wouldn't have met Smith. Had I not met Smith I wouldn't have caught his infectious love for learning—Often, when something in the gym needed repair, he would read how to do it, do it, and then teach a kid how to do it. You weren't around Smith very long before you got good at hammering nails, sawing boards and using paint brushes. Smith's only indulgence was taking voice lessons from a professional singer in Manhattan. He enjoyed singing and often sang while working around the gym. One of my fondest memories is of waking up at camp hearing Smith at the top of his voice sang "O What a Beautiful Morning", getting closer as he walked across the pasture headed for the kitchen.

The year I graduated from college I spent the summer working for Smith at Camp Glen Hardie. When summer ended, Smith drove me to Rochester, New York where I started medical school. On the way to Rochester he told me he wanted to show me a small piece of property he owned. He drove to a small cemetery in the countryside near Ithaca, New York. We got out of the car and walked a short distance to a ridge that overlooked a serene valley of farms and woodlands. "Look at that gorgeous view," he said. Then he proudly pointed to his cemetery plot. "That view is why I picked this spot," he said. "I'll lay up here and have that view forever." His words flowed without a hint of uneasiness. Smith always took pleasure in getting a job done, and done well.

Before starting my final year of medical school, my wife Nancy and I spent the summer at a small hospital in Le Ceiba, Honduras. Nancy volunteered as an obstetrical nurse while I learned about tropical diseases. At the end of the summer we had hoped to travel and see more of Central America, but did not have enough money. An interesting coincidence occurred a few days before we were to leave. I received a letter from Smith. It contained a check for several hundred dollars and a note saying that, unbeknownst to me, he had hoped to pay me more for that last summer at camp, but at the time did not have the funds.

Smith was always impacting lives. Long after settling into that hilltop near Ithaca, Smith continued impacting the lives of hundreds who used to be kids in a gym in Brooklyn.

CHAPTER 5

Joe

SMITH HAD A PART-TIME HELPER named Joe Murphy. Joe taught basic athletic skills, refereed basketball games and supervised the gym when Smith had to be away for a few hours. After watching our team play basketball at the Warren Street Community Center, Smith said we should get a coach. He told us to find Joe Murphy, and talk to him about it. Paddy, our team captain, and I found Joe, told him what Smith had said, and Joe agreed to coach our team.

Even from behind in a noisy, crowded gym, with kids racing around and balls flying through the air, you couldn't miss Joe. His mane of rowdy black curls spilled over his ears and down his neck to the top of his collar. He lived in baggy fatigue pants and wrinkled army surplus shirts. On cold days he added a heavy, coarsely knit, black wool sweater, an old companion with lots of miles on it. Most days his signature chin dimple remained hidden in a lawn of bristles. Joe was a hippie before there were hippies.

Joe came from a family of Irish prize fighters. His father had boxed, and Joe and both of his brothers followed in his footsteps, fighting for a while as amateur boxers. Drafted during World War II, Joe left Brooklyn a street-wise teenager with aspirations in the ring. He returned from the war an avowed pacifist, socialist and non-conformist. He also came back having made up his mind that he wanted to work with kids. With support from the G.I. Bill, Joe enrolled at Long Island University in a Social Work Program and took the job with Smith as a way to get some practical experience. After a few semesters Joe dropped out of school and the government checks stopped coming. He continued to work part-time at the gym and between the dollars he received from Smith and having a place to bunk on the top floor of a cold water flat owned by his brother-in-law, most of the time Joe got by, although sometimes he did odd jobs for extra money.

My mother didn't know Joe, but had seen him around the neighborhood. Once while walking with her I saw Joe across the street and waved. "How do you know that man?", she asked. "That's Joe Murphy. He's our basketball coach," I said.

Until I told her about Joe, she had thought he was a hobo. Downtown Brooklyn had a skid row whose contingents often drifted into our neighborhood. On bitter winter days tattered men could be seen in alleys and on vacant lots huddled around fires burning inside of discarded oil drums, their gaunt faces molded by years of loneliness and hard times, by demons from bottles in brown paper bags.

"Joe's a great guy," I said. "He goes to college. He fought in the War." My mother didn't reply. From her look I knew she was not ready to join the Joe Murphy Fan Club.

Joe had great rapport with kids. He spent hours watching us practice basketball, analyzing what we did when things worked, and when they didn't. During practice his face had an intensity that you never saw at other times.

Joe emphasized fundamentals: defense, hustle, passing, teamwork, shot selection, and his sacred grail—making foul shots. "If you're not using good form, it's worthless practicing foul shots," he said. "You should learn to shoot foul shots underhanded," he told us, "that's the best way." To our team that seemed bizarre. Joe went to the foul line, grasped the bottom of a basketball with his upturned palms and outstretched fingers, spread his legs, placed the ball between them, then bent his knees, squatted slightly, and in a single smooth motion stood up while lifting his arms and releasing the ball. It traveled in an arch that ended in the center of the hoop. It was the oddest-looking foul shot we had ever seen. One wiseacre whispered: "It looked like he's taking a crap."

"Hey Joe, people are going to laugh at us if we shoot that way," Paddy said with the rest of us nodding in agreement.

"Buddy Jeannette is the best foul shooter in professional basketball and that's the way he does it," Joe said. Nobody on our team had ever heard of Buddy Jeannette, or ever seen a professional basketball game. "The next time Baltimore plays the Knicks at Madison Square Garden, we'll go and you can see how he does it."

The local police station had a community juvenile officer from whom kids could get free tickets to sporting events. It was part of a city program called the Police Athletic League, designed to promote good relations between kids and cops. We got tickets and on a Saturday afternoon ten ragamuffins and a hippie rode the "A-train" to Madison Square Garden to study Buddy Jeannette's form.

We arrived early to find our seats and watch the teams warm up. At each end of the court basketballs flew through the air. Except for mid-flight collisions, it seemed almost every shot taken swished through the net. Minutes before game time fans occupied almost everyone of the Garden's 17,000 seats. We sat high in the balcony in a section loaded with kids seeing the game courtesy of the police department. After a silent pause for the national anthem, the Garden exploded with shouts, hoots, whistles and horns and as the referee lifted the ball for the tip off, you could feel the balcony vibrate from the crescendo of hand clapping and foot stomping. Each time Buddy Jeanette went to the foul line, we were all eyes. He made every foul shot. Back at the gym we practiced the Buddy Jeanette shot but by season's end only two players had perfected it. The rest of us reverted to our old ways and whenever we had a bad night at the foul line Joe would shake his head and remind us about Buddy Jeanette.

Sometimes a few of us would go to Joe's place to talk basketball. He lived with his brother Frank on the top floor of a wooden, three-story cold water flat owned by his brother-in-law, a hard working longshoreman not enamored with Joe's lifestyle. To describe Joe's place as unkempt failed to capture the extent of its clutter and disarray. Newspapers, sports magazines, empty cardboard coffee cups, food-stained paper plates and scrunched food wrappings from the Greek restaurant around the corner carpeted the floor of what passed as a living room. A small electric hot plate plugged into a wall outlet sat on a table in one corner. Except for a picture of Gandhi torn from a magazine and thumb tacked to a wall, Joe's place was testimony to indifference — an old sneaker here, a dirty towel there, a sweaty shirt on a doorknob, window shades that never raised, and permeating everything the smells of old coffee and stale cigarette smoke.

Surrounded by clutter in the middle of the living room sat a large corrugated metal basin containing layers of wet newspapers. Assuming the basin was for trash, my teammate Paddy once took an end stage wad of chewing gum from his mouth and pitched it into the basin. "Hey, don't throw that there," yelled Joe's brother Frank, "that's our fridge." Paddy retrieved the gum, squashed it into a piece of newspaper and placed it in his pocket. Frank lifted the wet newspapers in the basin to rearrange them, exposing a block of ice upon which sat strips of bacon, slices of salami, and assorted items of food. In the recess next to the block of ice sat a cardboard container of milk.

Joe and his bachelor brother spent the minimum on amenities. Once my teammate Eddie had to use the bathroom and when he finished, he couldn't find any toilet paper. When Eddie shouted out his predicament, Joe walked across the room, pushed the toilet door open and tossed Eddie a copy of Ring Magazine he had just retrieved from the living room floor.

***

I got to know Joe a lot better at summer camp. Joe spent two summers as head counselor at Camp Glen Hardie, a boys camp directed by Smith in the foothills of the Catskill Mountains, about 50 miles north of New York CityI went there as a camper and spent summers there as a counselor while in College. Joe rarely talked about his past, and never talked about his future. He seemed content to live life one day at a time. In contrast to his housekeeping at home, Joe was a stickler for keeping camp clean and tidy. Every day beds had to be made up, tent platforms swept, and the camp grounds policed to remove litter. After meals he made sure we cleaned the kitchen, washed and dried the dishes and utensils, scrubbed the pots and pans, and put everything in order for the next meal.

Joe served in many roles at Camp Glen Hardie. He umpired the softball games, served as lifeguard at the swimming hole, told stories around the evening campfire, supervised our daily chores, and chauffeured one of the camp vehicles when we went on field trips. Once we went to the Baseball Hall of Fame at Cooperstown, New York. Smith drove five boys in the camp station wagon and Joe took me and four others in a dilapidated 1938 Chevrolet panel truck that lacked side panels and back doors. The truck served around camp to haul gravel, lumber, cinder blocks and other materials for a building being built by Smith and several teenage boys from our neighborhood.

The drive to Cooperstown took three hours. Manny, the youngest camper sat in the passenger seat next to Joe munching on a large bag of marshmallows. The rest of us sat on the floor behind them. To prevent anyone from falling out of the back, a crisscross patchwork of ropes covered the opening created by the missing doors. The openness of the panel truck made riding in it an experience that was windy, noisy and full of exhaust fumes from our truck and the passing vehicles.

It was a cool, cloudy morning and about half way to Cooperstown, Willie, who was sitting with his legs hanging out the back of the truck, cried out: "Hey Joe, it's snowing!" Flecks of white flew past him, some brushing his neck and the side of his face. Excited, he turned around only to see Manny, who had become carsick, leaning out the passenger window, spewing digested marshmallows into the air.

As we approached Cooperstown, a wrong turn sent us down a dead-end road that stopped at a farmhouse. A man came out of an outbuilding and approached the panel truck, a look of curiosity on his face. Joe said: "I'll ask this guy how to get to the Baseball Hall of Fame." Before Joe could get it out, the man—who had been studying the grungy panel truck and its crew as he approached—looked at us and asked: "Are you all here to pick beans?" Joe explained we weren't migrant workers, then got directions from the farmer.

Joe had a small camera and took pictures of us at the Hall of Fame. When I returned from camp that summer I proudly showed my mother a picture of me standing in front of Babe Ruth's locker. Her immediate reaction was: "What's that behind your ear?" Until she asked, I hadn't noticed the cigarette. In the 1940s parking a cigarette behind the ear reflected the height of coolness among Brooklyn teenage boys. My mother knew what was parked behind my ear before she asked, she had been after me to stop smoking since I was 13. "It's going to stunt your growth and when you're old you won't have any wind," she would tell me.

Joe coached our team for two years. He loved teaching kids and being in a place where his appearance and political views didn't matter. He enjoyed being with Smith discussing government, politics and social issues. Cynical about much in society, and out on the streets a tough mug when he had to be, around kids in the gym Joe had a gentle, caring and positive touch. When he told us he couldn't coach any longer, he helped us find a new coach. After Joe stopped taking classes at Long Island University, the G.I. Bill checks stopped coming and he began spending less time at the gym. He started to lose some of his spark and when you talked with him he often seemed preoccupied. Looking back I realize that Joe was beginning to show signs of clinical depression. Joe and his brother Frank had returned from World War II convinced that ordinary people who went to work every day were victims of a system that kept poor people poor, and rich people rich. Having no interest in joining that system, they joined what Frank called "The 26/20 Club."

In New York in the 1940s, an unemployed person who had not quit their job, became eligible to receive $20 a week for up to 26 weeks. Twenty dollars wasn't a bad allowance with the minimum wage 75 cents an hour and cigarettes 17 cents a pack. To receive benefits required showing up once a week at the New York State Unemployment Office, standing in a long line to log in, then sitting in a large hall most of the morning waiting for your number to be called. Then you met your case worker who reviewed your history and handed you a list of job openings to pursue.

When Joe or Frank interviewed for a job, their garb, demeanor, and work records virtually guaranteed continued unemployment. When 26 weeks passed and the checks stopped coming, Joe would coast for a while, but when money got tight again, he'd find work as an unskilled laborer, usually in a warehouse, on a loading dock, or somewhere on the waterfront. After working for a few months he would figure out a way to get laid off, and then rejoin the "26/20 Club." They indulged in various penny ante schemes aimed at producing income without working. They bet on horse races, but lost more than they won. Before an afternoon at the track they spent evenings analyzing the records of race horses and jockeys, studying scratch sheets and plugging all that information into what they called "their system".

At the race track they spent the time between races down on hands and knees, searching through the carpet of tickets on the ground, hoping to find a mistakenly discarded winner. Rarely they found one, but never hit a bonanza.

They bet on professional boxing matches. Joe and Frank commanded encyclopedic knowledge of the fighting game. Having the luxury of lots of free time, they regularly visited the clubs in the city where fighters trained, and where the Murphys did their homework. They kept lists of each fighter's strengths and weaknesses. Were they in shape? Were they training seriously? Did they have a smart manager? How was there footwork? Could they take a good body punch? Did they have a glass jaw? After Joe stopped coaching our team, several of us continued to do things with him. Some Friday evenings we went to the boxing matches at Madison Square Garden with him and his brother Frank. Once in a while the Murphys hit a bonanza betting on a fight. Over time I learned about the dangerous scheme they used to win big. Gambling at the boxing matches had an odd feature. Wagering took place not only before the match began, but even after it ended, right up until the official winner was announced. The Murphy gimmick worked because when they placed their bets at the end of the fight, they already knew who had won.

Three officials, a referee and two judges, scored each fight. The two judges sat at ringside on opposite sides of the ring. At the end of every round each of the three officials independently decided which fighter had won the round and then marked their scorecards. Joe and Frank's balcony seats, one at either end of the arena, placed a Murphy behind and above each of the two judges. Using binoculars and their intimate knowledge of boxing, they could determine how each judge scored the fight as it progressed.

The third official, the referee, went to a corner of the ring to mark his card at the end of each round. Regardless of where he stood, one of the Murphy brothers could usually see the referee's card. Through the binoculars they couldn't read the print, but they could see which of the two columns on the card the official marked. It was pretty straight forward to deduce which column belonged to which fighter.

With subtle hand signals and binoculars, Joe and Frank communicated their findings to each other, and then placed bets. They used the scheme sparingly, waiting for a fight when the hoots and chatter around them left no doubt who the crowd thought had won, but Joe and Frank knew that the crowd was wrong. Strong opinions in the crowd meant getting higher odds betting against them. When the announced winner wasn't the fighter the crowd thought had won, it translated into a big payoff for the Murphy brothers. Had some of the rough hombres in the crowd learned of the fraud, it could have translated into a life-threatening situation for Joe and Frank. Whenever I was at the Garden on a night when they used their scheme, I feared that some bruiser would discover the scam and pitch a Murphy from the balcony into the seats below.

Over the years I lost track of Joe and Frank. Once while back in Brooklyn, I ran into Joe not having seen him for 20 years. Except for the long hair—now snowy white, and some wrinkles, he looked much the same. He asked where I lived. I told him in Iowa and gave him my address. When I asked where he lived, he said: "A lot of different places. I follow the ponies." He went on to explain.

He lived at race tracks up and down the East coast earning his keep by cleaning stables, and exercising horses. During winters the horses raced in Florida. When Spring came the races moved to tracks further north reaching New York in the summer. When fall arrived the races moved south completing the annual cycle in Florida. A year before he died I received a letter from Joe postmarked from a race track in Florida. He wrote about his life in the stables. I knew from the letter's tone that being around horses every day had been good medicine for my old coach. I wondered if finding a life with horses had saved him from becoming another gaunt figure huddled around an oil drum somewhere, trying to stay warm.

CHAPTER 6

Camp Glen Hardie

Every June, Smith closed the gym for three months and spent the summer directing Camp Glen Hardie, the Community Center's camp in the foothills of the Catskill Mountains, about a two-hour drive north of New York City. To city kids, going to Smith's camp was discovering a new world. Some kids said it was like going to heaven. At the camp kids swam everyday, and learned to ride a horse, row a boat, catch fish, and use a hatchet to cut wood and build a campfire.

Groups of about a dozen kids spent ten days at camp. Every tenth day during July and August excited kids and their mothers gathered on the sidewalk in front of the gym, waiting for Smith, Joe Murphy, and the returning campers to arrive in the camp's two station wagons. Shouts went up when the vehicles turned the corner at the far end of Warren Street and came into view. As the returning campers unloaded their gear they couldn't wait to tell the moms and kids on the sidewalk about their adventures at camp—about horses that wouldn't stop, skunks outside the tent at night, snakes and snapping turtles at the swimming hole, hornets in the outhouse. Each returning camper had two sacks for their mom –one filled with fresh vegetables from Smith's garden, the other filled with dirty clothes. Sometimes a kid returned with almost all of his clothes still clean, having changed outfits only sparingly during ten days away from maternal scrutiny.

As Smith and Joe oversaw the loading of the departing campers and their gear, a flurry of last minute instructions rained on the campers from the sidewalk.

"Make sure you brush your teeth!"

"Don't lose that good blanket!"

"You better not smoke any cigarettes!"

Then the station wagons pulled away. Camp was a bargain for neighborhood families. They paid five dollars per child for ten days at camp and if they couldn't afford to pay, camp was free. For some kids the drive to camp was the first time they had ever been out of Brooklyn. For some, the drive through the tunnel under New York Harbor was the first time they realized they lived on an island. In two hours they went from the sounds of trolley cars, fire sirens and horns to the sounds of birds, cicadas and tree frogs.

Camp Glen Hardie got its name from the Hardie family who donated the land, and from a glen on the property where a spring-fed brook cut through woodlands of shagbark hickory, paper birch and cedar. The first summer I went there I had just turned 14. I bunked with four buddies from our basketball team in a khaki canvas army-surplus tent that sat on a wooden platform in the woods. Most mornings we played softball in a rolling pasture at the edge of a crab apple orchard. A ball hit over the centerfielder's head into the orchard almost guaranteed a home run because it took time to find a ball hidden in the undergrowth of poison ivy that buzzed with yellow jackets attracted by apples rotting on the ground. Once in the middle of a game I retrieved a softball from under an apple tree hoping to throw the hitter out at home plate. As I put my fingers around the ball and wound up to throw it, I felt the sting of a yellow jacket right in the middle of my palm. The ball flew out of my hand and landed back in the poison ivy behind me.

Yellow jackets, bumble bees, wasps, and hornets were new encounters for city kids the first time they went to camp. So were frogs, snakes, turtles, woodchucks, and chicken hawks. In our neighborhood in Brooklyn the wildlife consisted of stray cats and dogs, pigeons, and an occasional rat that crawled out of a sewer opening. Yellow jackets were regular lunchtime visitors since peanut butter and jelly sandwiches were always on the menu and we ate meals on an open porch. One day at lunch the kid sitting across the table from me tumbled backwards off his chair, let out a horrendous scream, and grabbed his face after taking a bite of his sandwich. When he had made the sandwich and spread the grape jelly onto his bread, he hadn't noticed the yellow jacket that had found its way into the jelly jar.

Nights we sat around a campfire roasting marshmallows and listening to Smith tell stories. As he spoke some campers poked at the glowing coals with a stick, stopping from time to time to slap at mosquitoes that buzzed near their ears. There were always some campers who fussed about the bats that zigzagged overhead convinced one would swoop down and get caught in their hair. Some nights you could hear the calls of an owl or a coyote off in the distance. Smith told us that the local Ramapo Indians believed those sounds came from the ghosts of Skunimunk, an ancient Ramapo chief. The first time I ever saw the milky way, the big dipper and a shooting star was one moonless night after the camp fire went out and I lay in a pasture looking straight up. The sky seemed enormous and unreal. In Brooklyn the night time sky was an overhead slot between the walls of buildings where sometimes we saw the moon, but never saw constellations or shooting stars.

Smith took us on many field trips. Once we went to a county fair and saw kids our age—sometimes even girls—leading Holstein bulls on halters, something that seemed the ultimate in courage to a city kid. Another day we packed peanut butter and jelly sandwiches and

Kool Aid and spent an afternoon climbing to the top of Mohonk Mountain near New Paltz, New York. As we hiked the trail Smith talked about the wildflowers and trees, and when we reached the top he told us how glaciers 10,000 years before had carved out the valley we looked out on. Another time we went to General Knox's headquarters near West Point where Marquis de Lafayette had stayed one night around the time of the Revolutionary War. In a guest room of the house Smith showed us a window that had a woman's name scratched into one the panes of glass. He said that Lafayette had scribed the woman's name with his diamond ring after being taken by her beauty when he met her at dinner there that was attended by George Washington.

Once we went to the Baseball Hall of Fame at Cooperstown, New York. Joe Murphy took a picture of me standing in front of Babe Ruth's locker. I was so proud of the photo that when I returned home I showed it to my mother. She looked at the photo and knowing the answer before she even asked—she had a habit of asking those kinds of questions—she said, "What's that behind your ear?" Until that moment I hadn't noticed the cigarette. In the 1940s parking a cigarette behind one of your ears was a sign of coolness among Brooklyn teenage boys.

The facilities at Camp Glen Hardie were rustic, and while none of us came from pampered backgrounds, for us city boys camp took some getting used to. Water was pumped by hand from a well; candles, flashlights and Coleman lanterns provided the light at night; and even though some kids tried to hold out for ten days, everyone eventually learned to use the outhouse. Some even learned to sit in the outhouse instead of squatting, an adaptation that required breathing instead of trying to get in and out while holding your breath. A hearty few even learned to ignore the hornets' nest overhead and while waiting for nature to take its course, would sit and thumb through the Sears Roebuck catalogue that was there for backup in case the roll of tissue was empty. But most kids were in and out in a flash without their butts ever touching wood lest the black widow spider rumored to live down in the pit find some flesh. Kids were candidates for the camp's hall of fame if they had the guts to walk from their tent down through the woods to use the outhouse in the middle of the night.

We goofed around in our tents late into the night, and since Smith was a light sleeper, he stayed in a cabin about a quarter of a mile away. Joe Murphy, the camp counselor, stayed with the campers. Mornings at camp started right after sunrise and were announced by the voice of Smith getting closer as he walked up the pasture singing "Oh! What a Beautiful Morning" at the top of his voice.

Camp Glen Hardie ran on a shoestring budget. Food staples such as powdered milk, flour, powdered eggs, peanut butter, cooking oil and blocks of Velveeta cheese were provided free to the camp by a State Agency, and Smith had a large garden where he grew corn, tomatoes, peppers, squash and other vegetables. The campers rotated responsibility for kitchen duty, policing the grounds, cleaning the tents, and weeding the garden. It was a camp tradition that you left the place in better condition than when you arrived, so towards the end of our stay each group of campers spent one-half of a day on some project. Being around Smith was a never-ending learning experience. Campers learned to cut logs with a two-person saw and cut grass with a scythe. You weren't around Smith very long before you got pretty good at using tools, sizing up jobs, and shoveling gravel to maintain the road into camp.

The summer before I joined the Navy, Smith hired me to help him at camp. The job called for versatility. Sometimes I did counselor work, like taking kids on overnight hikes. A favorite of mine was climbing to the top of a mountain about two miles from camp. Near the top was an entrance to an abandoned iron ore mine. After cooking franks and beans over a campfire, telling stories and counting shooting stars, we slept outside on the ground in our bed rolls, unless it rained when we slept inside the mine entrance. Next morning with fresh batteries in our flashlights we descended into the mine, explored the tunnels, and squeezed through openings that led into large caverns where clusters of bats hung from the ceilings high above mounds of guano on the floor.

Some days I did odd jobs like clearing brush and grooming trails. Sometimes when Smith took the kids on a field trip I would stay and work in the vegetable garden. I learned to operate a small Waverly tractor so I could till the ground between the rows of crops. Once while wearing only a bathing suit and sneakers as I walked behind the tractor the tilling forks pierced an underground nest of yellow jackets. As soon as I felt the initial stings I took off running but then realized the tractor was still moving on its own and was headed for the woods. I ran back to the tractor as yellow jackets swarmed all over me, taking out their anger on my trunk, limbs and head. I found the engine kill-button, pushed it, raced off to the swimming hole, and dove in. For a few days I looked like I was coming down with chicken pox.

Smith had taught me to drive, so some days I was the camp chauffeur. On Sundays I drove the kids into town so they could attend their religious services. Most of the campers were Catholic, but were more interested in getting into town than in going to church. When church services were over all the campers wanted to go to the local general store. That's when I was kept busy making sure they didn't help themselves to candy bars and cookies. Sometimes after I got everyone into the station wagon for the trip back to camp, I had to return to the store to return candy bars that I had not seen when they went into a kid's pocket.

When I was in college I spent each summer helping Smith at Camp Glen Hardie. In the first group of campers that summer a ten-year-old Puerto Rican boy everyone called Bingo asked me to give him a haircut. I'd never cut hair before, but I found some shears and obliged. Soon campers began arriving with notes from their moms requesting haircuts for their sons and I added free haircuts to my list of odd jobs. During the first summer Smith began construction of a two-story building to house a kitchen, dining hall, community room, garage, maintenance shop and a washroom with toilets for the campers. He knew that for the building to become a reality, it would have to be a *do-it-yourself* operation done on a shoestring budget. During the previous winter Smith had prepared for the undertaking by reading books on masonry, carpentry and structural foundations. He tapped the heads of contractors and tradesmen. When he was out driving if he saw a house under construction he would stop, look, and ask questions.

The project maintained momentum because some of the alumni of the gym used their vacation time and weekends to work on the building. When weather permitted the construction continued on weekends during the spring and fall. A few of the volunteers had some experience in construction, but most learned on the job from Smith. He had a knack for teaching how to organize a piece of work and get the job done. He had a mantra about tools. If you understood how a tool did what it did, you could make the tool do most of the work. Around Smith you didn't just grab a hammer and start swinging at a nail. With Smith using tools was not about muscle. It was about angles, timing, and body rhythms, about proper grips, about keeping tools sharpened and cleaned. Once one of Smith's nephews, a civil engineer, visited camp and after inspecting the construction commented that it seemed his uncle was expecting typhoons. The building was completed in two years.

At the end of the summer the year I graduated from the University of Missouri Smith drove me to Rochester, New York, where I started medical school. On the way to Rochester he told me he wanted to show me a small piece of property he had just purchased. He drove to a small cemetery out in the country near Ithaca. We got out of the car and walked a short distance to a hilltop that overlooked a serene valley of farms and woodlands. "Look at that gorgeous view," he said. Then he proudly pointed to his cemetery plot. "I picked this spot because of that view," he said. When I graduated he drove to Rochester to attend. That was the last time I saw him. Twenty five years later Nancy and I visited his grave site. The view from the hilltop had changed, gone was the pastoral scene, in its place a suburban housing development.

Smith enriched the lives of hundreds of city kids. Some finished high school and went on to college and successful careers because of his influence. Some didn't go to prison because of his intervention at their court trials. If anyone ever lived each day by the golden rule, it was Smith.

CHAPTER 7

Brushes with Teeth
Dental Encounters in a Brooklyn Childhood

EVERY MORNING UNTIL I WAS ABOUT nine years old, my mom lined the five of us up by the kitchen window. She said the light was better there. My two sisters, two brothers and I watched as she unscrewed the cap on the large brown bottle and carefully began to pour.

One by one, steadying a head with one hand and guiding her spoon past a pinched nose and a scrunched face with the other, she lifted a spoon to our lips and it was down the hatch with a slug of viscous, foul-smelling cod liver oil. "It's good for your bones and teeth," she would tell us. "You won't have to go to the dentist so often."

The dreaded "D word" could make our eyeballs roll. Few childhood experiences triggered more angst in us than being in a dental chair. Routine exams and preventive dental care, if they existed then, hadn't made their debut in our neighborhood. A trip to the dentist always meant trouble. It meant drilling and yanking without an anesthetic. It meant jaws wedged open by a device that protected dentists' fingers from children's incisors. For a kid the only pleasant dental experience was finding a nickel under your pillow the morning after placing a tooth there.

The teeth of grownups also had a bedroom connection. Some people my parents' age, and most people my grandma's age, kept a glass of salt water next to their beds. Before turning out the lights at night, they removed their teeth and placed them in the glass. This maneuver served to clean their false teeth and to help avoid choking on them if they came loose while they slept.

Family lore abounded with dental tales. Our dad told us about outdoor dentistry. When he was a kid dentists made the rounds of city neighborhoods in horse-drawn wagons. When someone with a bad tooth came forward, the dentist performed the extraction or filling with the patient sitting in a chair up on the wagon, while the horse rested and munched oats. The proceedings attracted spectators who watched from the sidewalk as the dentist yanked a tooth or whittled away on one with a treadle-powered drill.

When I had a toothache, my mother reached for the vial of clove oil she kept with the iodine, mercurochrome, argyrole, musterole, witch hazel, oil of wintergreen, bottles of various liniments, and other remedies on the top shelf of the pantry. It was also where she kept the cod liver oil.

When I was 11, my teacher sent me home one day because I had an piercing toothache. My mom usually treated toothaches with a dab of clove oil on a piece of cotton. Placing it on the aching tooth often reduced the pain. At night the moaning of a kid with a toothache created a problem when five children and two adults slept in two adjoining rooms. One night the clove oil failed, and it was out of bed and off to the kitchen. There my mom poured a half cup of table salt into a skillet, placed it on the stove and lit a fire. When the salt grains got so hot they began dancing in the skillet, she poured the salt into a sock, tied a knot at the top, and placed it over the aching tooth. "It'll bring more blood to your tooth and make the pain go away," she said after placing the sock on my cheek.

In an instant, the side of my face felt on fire. "Now, keep it there! Don't take it off," she said. The pain on my cheek took my mind off the toothache—*distraction therapy* at its best.

The clove oil didn't help that day the teacher sent me home. My mother phoned a neighborhood dentist who told her to send me over. I walked the two short blocks to his office which was located one floor above a saloon and two floors above the neighborhood subway station. The door from the street opened to a steep, narrow flight of stairs. At the top was a tiny waiting room, and beyond that was a small room with a dental chair. To the left of the chair was a door leading to a small laboratory. Through the door I saw a white-coated technician sitting at a bench holding what looked like a small ceramic model of teeth in one hand and picking at it with a tiny wire brush held in the other. A small lathe sat on the bench.

The dentist gestured toward the chair and I climbed into it. As the dentist began examining my teeth, the technician made the first of several appearances at the dentist's side. Each time, the technician arrived with a set of false teeth in hand, seeking an assessment of the them and further instructions. From his seat on the stool, the dentist looked back over his shoulder, had the technician hold the teeth nearer the overhead lamp, examined them from different angles, and said a few words. Then the technician disappeared back into the laboratory.

As the dentist probed and picked inside of my mouth, I flinched each time a tool or a stream of water touched my aching tooth. While he worked, rumbling sounds and vibrations percolated up through the building as subway trains came and went. This early in the day, all was quiet in the saloon one floor below us.

After a few minutes, the dentist said he had to pull the tooth. He took a chemical that smelled like oil of clove and applied it to the aching tooth in my lower jaw. He then set about to remove the tooth using a tool that looked like a fancy set of pliers. My hands gripped the arms of the chair, my fingers squeezing and locking on like the jaws of a snapping turtle on the head of a fish. The dentist grasped the tooth with the pliers, twisted and pulled, then pushed and pulled, and then twisted again. The tooth didn't budge. He tried again several times, but without success. The pain got worse. After several attempts, he stopped and looked up.

From the maze of elbow-hinged mobile arms suspended from the ceiling, he pulled down an arm that had a narrow, chisel-shaped instrument attached to its free end. Long wire cables the width of shoe laces connected the instrument in his hand to a small motor mounted on the hinged arm. He told me he needed to loosen the tooth, and placed the tip of the instrument against it. When he started the motor a staccato burst of shocks knocked the tooth, each shock sounding like a rock hitting a rock. With each burst from what seemed like a miniature pile driver, my jaw vibrated like a tuning fork and a bolt of pain pushed me back in the chair.

After several attempts to loosen the tooth, he put the instrument aside and again picked up the shiny pliers. He grasped the tooth with them, and pulled. Out came the tooth—at least I thought it did. The pain persisted and my jaw felt like Joe Louis had landed one on it. The dentist probed the tooth's crater triggering sharp pains each time his tool made contact.

"The roots broke off," he said. "I need to do some more work to get them out."

Not knowing what was next, my fear increased. Each time he touched the site where my tooth had been, a jolt of pain shot through my jaw and I lurched away. My spastic movements interfered with his efforts, and after a couple of tries, he stepped back, packed the area with gauze, and disappeared through the laboratory door.

I could hear him speaking on the phone, but I couldn't understand most of what he said. I knew he must be talking with my mother who was home with a sick baby. I heard the word *surgeon*, and I started to panic. I had visions of someone cutting out a piece of my jaw.

When he returned from the phone he told me I needed to go to another dentist, an oral surgeon, who would remove the roots. He led me down the stairway and stepped into the street, where he waved down a passing taxi. He put me into the back seat of the cab, gave the cabbie instructions, and handed him some money.

As the cab made its way through the streets, I sat in the back holding the side of my throbbing jaw and looking out the side window. The cab moved along at a good clip, but the cabbie didn't speak. After about ten minutes I had no idea where we were. Fixated on the word surgeon and without any idea what was in store for me, my panic turned to terror.

Finally, the cab stopped at a side entrance of the Williamsburg Savings Bank Building, the tallest building in Brooklyn—a landmark I knew. Recognizing the building triggered a transient flash of relief. As the cab pulled up, a woman who stood in the doorway of the building came forward. In a moment she had me in an elevator climbing to an upper floor of the building. When the elevator doors opened, she whisked me into a large dental suite and helped me into a much fancier dental chair than the one I had left twenty minutes before.

A man and two women, each dressed in white, entered the room. The man said he was Dr. Callahan and the two nurses were his assistants. He told me he was going to fix my tooth, but first he had to put a mask over my face to put me to sleep. He said I wouldn't feel anything and when I woke up everything would be fixed. My tooth and jaw ached and I felt frightened because I didn't know anyone in the room.

One of the nurses placed a green apron over my chest. Dr. Callahan reclined my chair and gently placed a soft, black rubber mask over my nose and mouth. I heard the hissing sounds of gas moving through the snaky coils connected to the mask and began to smell something medicinal. Across my mind flashed the terrifying thought that I might not wake up. I began to feel groggy, and as much as I tried, I couldn't stay focused on what would happen to me if I didn't wake up. As the nitrous oxide put me further down, I had the sensation of floating in air, moving away and getting smaller, like a kid's balloon when the string is let go.

I looked beyond the rim of the mask and saw the blue eyes, blond hair, and beautiful smiling face of a nurse looking down at me. Then I felt her take my left hand, gently pat the back of it, and give a reassuring nod. I felt safe, and then I was gone.

I awoke on a couch, alone in a dimly lit room. The tooth was gone, the pain was gone, and the beautiful nurse was gone. Soon a secretary entered and told me my aunt was coming to take me home.

I've often wondered whether the beautiful nurse was real or the creation of a terrified kid's mind with the help of some nitrous oxide. Either way, some vivid images got hardwired in my cortex as I faded away in the dental chair that afternoon. Countless times during the ensuing sixty years I've thought about the safe feeling I had when she touched my hand. I can still close my eyes and see her smile.

CHAPTER 8

Pocket Money

My FATHER'S CONVICTION THAT "You don't get nothing for nothing in this world," translated into a policy of not giving his children an allowance. This policy vaulted pocket money into second place, only behind basketball, on my list of teenage priorities. Generating money involved a hodge-podge of constantly changing activities. Sometimes I painted rooms in apartment houses with Joe Walsh, a cheery Irishman who supported himself doing odd jobs because his weakness for the suds that flowed from the taps at O'Hagen's saloon undermined steady employment. Sometimes I provided grunt for Ray Bashara, a burly Syrian neighbor who earned money moving households. And sometimes I set pins in one of downtown Brooklyn's bowling alleys.

Automatic pin-setting machines, if they existed, had not yet arrived in Brooklyn in the late 1940s. Most bowling alleys had at least twelve lanes. Setting pins was a one-night-at-a-time job with no paper work involved. You earned 12 cents per game plus tips at a time when cigarettes sold for 17 cents a pack. The first time you showed up at an alley looking for work, the manager would look you over, ask a few questions and if he liked what he saw and heard, he would tell you to stick around for a while. Then if some of the skid row characters who usually set pins hadn't arrived by the time bowlers were ready to roll, you had a job for that night.

Setting pins was a noisy, hazardous way to earn a few dollars. On weekday nights a bowling alley bustled from just before dinner time till about 10 p.m. The pin setter worked in a pit at the end of the alley. When a ball collided with the ten pins, the pins became airborne, some ricocheting off the sidewalls and flying into the pit along with the bowling ball. From the ceiling above the pit a metal bar hung that allowed you to swing up and out of the way in a maneuver borrowed from the ape house at the zoo. Or you could jump up onto a narrow wooden board mounted on the back wall of the pit, high enough that once you were on it, you were relatively safe.

After the ball and pins crashed into the pit, you dropped down, grabbed the ball, shoved it into a gully that returned the ball to the bowler, and then hustled to reset the wooden pins. Resetting the pins required coordinating your eyes and four limbs while keeping both ears and the eyes in the back of your head attuned to the action in the pits to your right and left. You stood on one foot and used the other to depress a treadle that elevated a triangular array of ten metallic pegs. The 3-inch pegs fit into cylindrical slots in the bottom of the wooden pins. Grabbing two wooden pins with each hand, you rapidly placed a pin on each of the metallic pegs. If the pins weren't seeded squarely, when you released the foot treadle and the metallic pegs retracted, a pin would topple, knocking over others and requiring you to reset everything, meaning the bowler had to wait. Bowlers don't like waiting. The longer they wait, the unhappier they get. The unhappier they get, the smaller they tip. The longer they wait, the fewer games that get played. The fewer games that get played, the less money that goes into the establishment's till. Waiting made everyone unhappy. You learned to work fast in the pit. In order to make it worth your while, you needed to simultaneously set pins on two adjacent lanes. Adjacent pits were separated by a short wall with an opening for the pin setter to move from one pit to the other. Sometimes when you were setting pins in one lane, pins from the other lane would come flying at you through the opening before you had a chance to grab the metal bar above and move out of the way. You got good at dodging flying pins.

When I was 15, one of my best friends was a Puerto Rican boy named Angelo. Everyone, including his mother, father, brothers, and sisters called him Spicky. Even though "Spicky" was usually considered a derogatory term, the name never bothered Angelo until he reached seventeen. Then he let everyone know that he wanted to be called Angelo and from then on, out on the street, he was Angelo. But even a year later, when his mother answered the door and I asked for Angelo, she said, in broken English through a partial harelip: "No, Spicky's not here."

Angelo was a master at "junking," the scavenging of abandoned buildings. After World War II, New York City condemned a large neighborhood near the Brooklyn Navy Yard in order to build an enormous, low rent, high-rise public housing complex. After the old buildings had been vacated they remained empty for almost a year, except for hobos who used the deserted buildings as places to crash for the night or to stay dry when it rained. For me and Angelo junking involved rummaging through those abandoned buildings harvesting lead pipes and copper gutters, cutting or bending them into pieces that fit into gunny sacks, and then selling the metal at one of the junk yards on Third Avenue. One summer day I went junking with Angelo, and after we had loaded our sacks and were hustling along Fulton Street, moving along at a good clip with the sacks over our shoulders, I spied my Aunt Margaret on the other side of the busy street. I was pretty sure she didn't see me, but if she had, I knew that the first words out of her mouth would have been, "What's in the sack?"

When I got home that evening my mother said: "Your Aunt Margaret saw you running down Fulton Street this afternoon." At this point I knew I was dead meat. My mom continued: "Your Aunt said you looked filthy, your clothes were all dusty, your hair was a mess and there was a hole in the back of your pants." I looked at my mother as I searched for a response to what I knew would come next. But next never came. My mother never mentioned a sack. I'd been saved by Aunt Margaret's obsession with outward appearances.

Once Angelo asked me to sleep over because his father needed some help moving an old sofa-bed. Angelo's father was a merchant seaman, a bit of a rooster and fond of the spirits. He would be gone for months at a time, return home for a week or so, and then be off again. Angelo told me that his father had purchased a new sofa-bed that was scheduled for delivery the next day and he needed help getting rid of the old one because the company refused to take it without being paid extra. The dark, narrow hallways, tight corners, and four flights of steep stairs between the street and the fourth floor apartment made the company's position reasonable, but Angelo's father was looking for a cheaper solution.

Angelo's family lived in a three-room apartment on the top floor of an old tenement building on Wyckoff Street. His parents slept in one room and the six children slept in what during the day was the living room and at night became two sleeping spaces, a drape separating the boys from the girls. The third room was a small kitchen. Since I'd been invited for overnight, I fell asleep assuming that we would be moving the piece of furniture the next morning. In the middle of the night Angelo's father woke us, and said it was time to move the sofa-bed. At first I thought he was drunk, but then I realized he was totally sober. As Angelo and I put on our shoes, his father woke the other boys and sent the two youngest ones into the parents' bedroom. Partially awake, I said to myself: "Something's crazy here. We can't be moving a piece of furniture in the middle of the night."

Leaving all the lights in the apartment unlit, Angelo's father took a screwdriver and began removing the child safety railing from one of the windows. When he finished he told Manny, the oldest of Angelo's younger brothers, to go down to the street and make sure nobody was around. At that point I realized what was going on. Angelo's father removed the mattress and bedding from the old sofa-bed where Manny and his two younger brothers had been sleeping and then folded the frame and springs back inside of it. When Manny gave the all clear signal from down on the street, Angelo, his father, and I lifted the heavy sofa-bed, tilted it on its side, and carefully slid it onto the window sill. Angelo's father fretted about the bed opening and getting stuck in the window frame, a predicament that would have been difficult to deal with in the middle of the night. We got the bulky piece balanced on the window sill and on a whispered count of three we gave it a strong push, then stepped back. Two seconds later a thundering sound echoed in the street as the couch hit the flagstone sidewalk. Manny returned, Angelo's father shut the window and then disappeared behind a closed bedroom door. Angelo and I got under our covers, and Manny, his bed now deceased, spent the rest of the night on the old mattress on the floor.

From Angelo I got the idea of earning money by shining shoes. Angelo and several of my friends had shine boxes, so I decided to build one, get some polish, brushes, and shine cloths, and go into business. It was easy to find customers in saloons, at subway entrances, and outside the court houses and municipal buildings in downtown Brooklyn. After shining shoes for a few days I proudly showed my mother the money I had earned. She had a conniption. "I won't be having any child of mine shining shoes on the streets," she shouted. Her response came as a surprise, metaphorically grabbing me by the ankles in mid-stride. "Only kids from poor families shine shoes and I won't have you out advertising we're poor when we're not," she went on. I had never thought of our family as being poor. We ate three times a day, got clothes when we needed them, stayed warm in the winter, and went to a movie most weekends. To me my family wasn't poor, I was poor—and shining shoes seemed like a good solution. I could tell from my mother's stern look, the certainty of her tone, and the immediacy of her response that I was destined to lose any battle over shining shoes.

I knew my parents struggled to make ends meet because sometimes I overheard them talking about not being able to pay all the bills. My mother would be distraught about the situation and my father would say: "Well, let's pay everything except these three." Then my mother would say: "Jimmy, we can't do that! They'll have people at the front door wanting their money." My father would say: "Look, those three outfits won't starve if they don't hear from us for a month. We'll catch them next payday." My father's cavalier attitude caused my mother to fret even more.

The best job I had as a teenager was working Saturdays as a delivery boy at a delicatessen on Montague Street, in Brooklyn Heights. The starting wage was forty cents an hour, but sometimes you could make a dollar an hour because most people tipped quite generously. My older brother Jim worked in the deli and helped me get the job. Brooklyn Heights was a neighborhood filled with writers, artists, and professional people, some of them well known. It was not uncommon that the person answering the door when I made a delivery was someone I recognized from the newspaper or from seeing them on TV. One of my customers was Arthur Miller who wrote "Death of a Salesman." Another was Eugene Dennis, the Secretary General of the Communist Party of the United States, at the time charged with conspiracy to overthrow the government. He was ultimately convicted and served four years in federal prison.

Directly across from the delicatessen stood the Hotel Bossert, a Brooklyn Heights landmark. Some of the players and Burt Shotton, the manager of the Brooklyn Dodgers, lived in the Bossert.

Sometimes I would be loading my delivery cart and recognize that the fellow standing at the counter waiting to pay for his snacks was Preacher Roe or some other famous Dodger player. Once when I made a delivery and the customer let me into the apartment, I heard the voice of Red Barber, the play-by-play radio broadcaster of the Brooklyn Dodger baseball games. I assumed the voice came from a radio, but while I was unloading the groceries in the kitchen, I looked through the doorway to the living room and saw Red Barber himself sitting on a couch engaged in conversation.

After working in the deli for a while I realized that I was purposely being kept from making deliveries to certain customers. One customer's order was always delivered by Eddie, a handsome young Scandinavian fellow who worked full-time in the deli. Eddie would say: "Leave that order for me. I'll deliver it on the way home." I assumed that the customer must have been a great tipper. I later learned that the customer was a woman in her forties who had a weakness for young guys. Once on a particularly busy Saturday I found a load of groceries in my delivery cart marked for a long-time customer to whom I had never made a delivery. When I knocked on the apartment door, a friendly gentleman opened the door and told me to put the groceries on the table in the kitchen. It soon became clear that the gentleman had a fondness for young boys. Later I learned that my boss had told the other employees that because of my age I shouldn't be assigned deliveries to that customer. The groceries had been put in my delivery cart by mistake. After working at the deli for two years, new owners took over and I was laid off to make room for the teenage son of one of the new owners.

That summer Willie, one of my basketball teammates, told me about an opening in a printing firm in a building where his mom worked. I applied for the job, had an interview with the foreman, and got hired. The company occupied a huge loft on the top floor of a warehouse near the Brooklyn Bridge. The loft contained four massive printing presses that spewed out sheets of paper a bit longer and wider than a king-size mattress. Printed on each sheet were dozens of book pages oriented so that when the sheets were later cut and folded at a bindery they formed a cassette of pages that when bound together with cassettes of other pages and placed inside of a cover, formed a book. As each sheet came off the press it passed over a row of gas-burning jets that dried the ink before the sheet fell onto the growing stack of printed sheets on a wooden pallet . When the pallet was full, my job was to move it from the loft to the truck-loading dock located at street level six stories below. I moved the pallet using a skid that was essentially a manually-powered mini-fork lift. After I positioned the prongs of the fork under the pallet I used the hydraulic jack built into the handle of the skid to elevate the pallet so it now sat on the skid and the wheels of the skid were free to move.

Controlling the movement of a skid loaded with a half ton of paper required brute force. Pulling a loaded skid along a concrete floor filled with ruts was tricky business. When a wheel got stuck in one of the ruts, freeing the skid required a push and pull tug-of-war maneuver more suited for mule than man. I soon learned that the best way to avoid getting stuck was to keep the skid moving fast enough that momentum kept the skid moving even when one of its wheels hit a chuckhole. Navigating a fast moving skid around printing presses, concrete stanchions, and human traffic was unnerving at best. More than once I came close to upending a worker who suddenly appeared from behind a printing press carrying a cup of coffee or a five gallon drum of some chemical. But navigating the skid was tame compared to getting it onto the freight elevator and riding it down to street level. When I guided the front end of the loaded skid onto the elevator, the skid's weight caused the elevator car to descend several inches. Consequently, when the back wheels of the skid rolled off the floor of the loft, they free-fell several inches before crashing onto the car floor of the elevator. When the skid was completely aboard, the elevator car dropped an additional two inches and momentarily bobbed, as if suspended by rubber cables. Once I had the skid in place, I moved the elevator's control lever to the down position. As the elevator made its slow descent, its motor whining in the background, I mused about the possibility of the cable failing and an express ride to the bottom of the shaft. Until I gained experience, each time I stopped the elevator at ground level its floor was not aligned with the floor of the loading dock, a prerequisite for moving the loaded skid from the elevator. Getting the floors aligned required short pulses up or down on the elevator control lever, each pulse ending with the elevator car bobbing for a few seconds.

Besides the elevator, the job had other hazards. Several times each day a fire alarm sounded because a sheet coming off a press got jammed and burst into flames as it passed over the gas jets. Every worker had been trained to stop what they were doing, rush to the fire, and get the burning sheet away from the press. Using a fire extinguisher was out of the question because it could ruin the printed sheets already on the pallet and cause damage to the printing press. We were expected to get the burning sheet off the press and then stomp out the flames. Stomping out the flames was easy, but grabbing the paper often resulted in fine linear incisions on the fingers or palms. A fire in a loft filled with paper and organic solvents had the potential to quickly get out of hand and the most serious offense an employee could commit was failing to immediately rush to the site of a fire when the alarm sounded. The foreman was adamant that fires were to be handled without the involvement of the NYFD. Had the fire department been called, by the time they arrived the fire would have already been extinguished. Replaying that scenario dozens of times a month guaranteed reactions from the fire marshal that the firm wanted to avoid. Besides, if the fire department came each time there was a fire it would have meant innumerable work stoppages.

During the summer I worked there we never had a fire that got out of control because the employees responded immediately and handled the situation without causing damage to the presses or the printed sheets.

Soon after I began working at the firm I noticed that every morning a short, friendly, well-dressed gentleman appeared on the floor, stopping briefly to chat with some of the workers, frequently taking notes. I never met him but he seemed to know everyone in the place, so I assumed he was from management. Occasionally I saw him in the men's room where sometimes he gave me a friendly nod in passing. One day while washing my hands I happened to notice three numbers written in colored chalk on the wall above one of the sink's in the men's room. With time I began to realize that the chalked numbers changed every day. One day it might be 027, the next day 854, and the following day 382. At a coffee break I mentioned this to one of the press operators.

"Oh, that's the number," he said.

"What number?" I asked.

"The number. The winning number." My blank face told him I didn't know what he was talking about.

"You know Vinnie?" he asked. Another blank look.

"That guy who comes around every morning taking bets, that's Vinnie. He's a runner for a bookie. He writes yesterday's winning number on the wall in the men's room and Sissy, the secretary, she writes it for him on the wall in the ladies' room. It's the last three digits of the number of dollars bet at the race track yesterday. That number gets printed in the newspaper, so there can't be any cheating. You give Vinnie a dime, a quarter or a buck and he writes down the number you want. If your number comes up, you could win $500, depending on what you bet."

At the end of the summer I decided I had had enough of that job.

I had no idea what I wanted to do in life, but I knew I didn't want to work as an ape. I went to the foreman and told him told him I was quitting.

"Why are you leaving?' he asked.

I should have been polite, but being a flippant teenager I responded, "I don't see this job as having a future except for building muscles. You don't need a person to do it, you need a gorilla."

A look of surprise flashed across his face, then it softened into a hint of a smile and he said, "Kid, with an attitude like that you're never going to amount to anything in this world."

The following summer I worked for Smith at Camp Glen Hardie. When I returned home at the end of September my father's conviction that "you don't get nothing for nothing in this world" led me to the first job I ever had that was not driven by the need for pocket money. It was 1952, our country was fighting a war in Korea and I knew I would soon receive my draft notice. My father wanted me to find a job while I waited to be drafted, but I dragged my feet. After a few weeks, he issued an ultimatum: "You're not going to freeload here. You get a job and pay your share, or you move out!" I went to the post office and enlisted in the Navy for four years. I picked the Navy because of all the military services the Navy had the shortest wait before being inducted. I didn't appreciate it at the time, but my father's ultimatum was one of the best things that ever happened to me.

CHAPTER 9

A Short Visit Home

THE SIGN BY THE SIDE OF THE ROAD read "New York City 10 miles." Through the truck windshield I could make out the top of Manhattan's skyline. It had been almost two years since I had left the city. I'd never been away from home that long before. When I left I was 18, a high school drop-out who had just enlisted in the Navy for four years.

As the skyline got closer I thought about the brisk November morning two years before when I said goodbye to my family, grabbed the small gym bag I had packed the night before, and walked to the Warren Street station where I squeezed into a subway car loaded with rush-hour commuters headed for Manhattan. When the doors of the subway car opened at the Wall Street station I joined the human wave of men in suits and ties and neatly dressed women that poured out onto the platform and surged towards the stairs that led to the street. They headed for offices in the skyscrapers that lined the streets of lower Manhattan. In jeans, sneakers and a sweatshirt, I headed for the military induction center at 39 Whitehall Street, an address familiar to draft-age males in New York City. Surrounded by banks, stock markets and investment firms, the red granite, fortress-like Victorian structure where teenagers began the process of becoming soldiers and sailors was a financial district anomaly.

The hallways at 39 Whitehall were crowded with young men and I made my way to the floor designated for Navy recruits. After nine hours of psychological and aptitude tests, physical and mental exams, immunizations, and blood and urine tests, forty of us raised our right hands and took the oath. Each of us was issued dog tags and a military ID number, and appointed as a seaman recruit, the lowest rank in the Navy. Then the forty of us marched through downtown Manhattan, shepherded along by a salty Chief Petty Officer in spit-polished shoes, rows of multicolored campaign ribbons pinned to his neatly pressed jacket. On his left sleeve were six gold hashmarks, one hashmark for each of his four years of service. Nothing about the marching group—not their garbs, hairdos, postures, or gaits—hinted at anything military. We reached the Erie Lackawanna Terminal at the foot of Chambers Street, rode a ferry across the Hudson River to New Jersey, and boarded an overnight train headed for Chicago and our final destination, the Great Lakes Naval Training Center.

Now, two years later, I had come back to New York for a short visit, this time riding under the Hudson River through the Holland Tunnel in the cab of a tractor-trailer rig. Four days earlier, in Seattle, I had boarded a Greyhound bus headed for New York City. I had just completed 15 months on Kodiak Island, Alaska, and my request for two weeks of leave had been granted. On Kodiak I worked as a weatherman in a unit that forecasted the weather for military operatives in the Northern Pacific Ocean and the Arctic. As I watched Idaho, Montana, North Dakota, Minnesota and Wisconsin pass by, the wide open spaces outside my window made my small seat seem even smaller. On a map Montana looks wide; on a Greyhound before interstate highways, Montana seemed endless. After a disquieting four-hour experience early in the trip, each time the seat next to me became empty, I worried that its next occupant would be another oversized snorer. Trying to sleep on the Greyhound was like trying to sleep in a telephone booth where the phone keeps ringing. By day three I had a bad case of bus fever.

In 1954 Greyhounds did not have onboard facilities, and most rest stops across the northern Great Plains were at gas stations and diners in small towns. So every few hours when the bus made a brief stop, I had to make a choice. I could chose relief or nourishment. Relief came at the end of a long line to get into the men's room. Nourishment came at the end of a line that dawdled past cellophane-wrapped sandwiches and muffins and ended at the cashier. Sometimes the bus stopped long enough to make it through both lines.

Before the bus reached Chicago, I decided to get off there, cash in the rest of my ticket, and hitchhike to New York. I needed space. I knew that getting rides would be easy because I was dressed in a Navy uniform. Midway across Pennsylvania a trucker with a son in the Navy stopped and gave me a lift all the way into New York City. As I hopped down from the cab of his semi at a Manhattan street corner, I thanked him for the ride and for the breakfast at a truck stop in New Jersey, and headed for the subway. I was excited about seeing my family and some of my buddies.

On the second night home, dressed in civvies that had waited in a closet for two years, I walked to several neighborhood hangouts, hoping to find familiar faces. Living on Kodiak Island made the streets of Brooklyn seem tiny. After checking three taverns and not finding anyone my age, I began to wonder whether nobody was around because it was a weekday night or because there was a war in Korea and most guys my age were off in the military. Then I ran into Honey Walsh, a fellow a few years older than me who, in spite of being a heavy smoker and drinker since his early teens, had been one of the most gifted basketball players in our neighborhood.

"Honey, it's great to see you," I said. "I've been all around the neighborhood and you're the first guy I've run into who I know."

"Yeah, the neighborhood's pretty dead these days," he said. "Most of the guys you know are still in the service. I didn't get in because they said I was 4-F. When I went for my physical the doc heard a murmur and said that the rheumatic fever I had when I was a kid messed up my heart valves.

"Once in a while I see someone we knew from the old gym," he continued. "I ran into your buddy Leo a few weeks ago. He can't wait to get out of the Army. He's stationed in Texas and told me it's not a friendly place to be when you're black. He said in the town next to the base they have separate everything's for whites and blacks."

Leo and I had been classmates since first grade at St. Paul's elementary school. I knew that Leo wouldn't like being in the South. His family came from Barbados and considered themselves different from their black neighbors on Wyckoff Street, almost all of whom came to Brooklyn from places like South Carolina and Georgia. Leo used to tell me, "My family didn't pick cotton in Alabama or Mississippi." But out on the street, be it in Brooklyn or anywhere, the world treated Leo as just one more black guy.

"There are a lot more Puerto Ricans in the neighborhood now," Honey said. "A lot of them don't even speak English. It used to be that Atlantic Avenue had lots of Syrian and Lebanese, now it's mostly Puerto Rican. You know that big Middle Eastern grocery store on Atlantic near Court Street, now it's a Puerto Rican Evangelical Church. Speaking about Atlantic Avenue, now that I think of it," Honey went on, "you might find some people you know down at Red Mike's, that bar down near the docks at the end of Atlantic. For some reason the place became a popular hangout for some people. I might even go down there myself later tonight."

I left Honey and headed for Red Mike's. The place was crowded, noisy, and reeked of cigarette smoke. There were more girls than you usually find in an Irish bar and two of them were dancing in front of a juke box that was playing the Demarco Sisters singing "Time don't change a thing." I looked around and recognized that the bartender was Porky, the oldest brother of my friend Eddie. In his younger days Porky had been a professional fighter, but now, after years of drinking and hard living, he no longer relied on his fists to deal with the occasional unruly customer; he kept a baseball bat behind the bar for that job.

"Hi, Porky," I said. "How's Eddie?"

"He's in the Army stationed in Germany. He lucked out. They didn't send him to Korea."

"How's your family?" I asked. "Well, my father—God have mercy on his soul—passed away last year, but everyone else is okay."

I remembered Eddie's father well. He was a strikingly handsome man off the boat from Ireland, quick with strong opinions on almost anything and always delivered in a loud, thick brogue. He worked as a waiter in a fancy Manhattan restaurant. He stood out even on a crowded Brooklyn street as he traveled to and from work each day dressed in formal attire. He purchased one of the first television sets in our neighborhood. I often pestered Eddie for an invitation to watch a Brooklyn Dodgers baseball game on his father's TV set. Our family didn't have a TV. Eddie said his father didn't like being disturbed while he watched a baseball game. Even at mealtime around the family table, Eddie and his brothers and sister were not allowed to talk unless spoken to by their father. Eddie promised to ask his father, but warned that if I came to watch a game I had to sit still and not talk. Then one day Eddie told me I could come to watch a game. The night of the game I climbed the hallway stairs of the tenement building to the second floor apartment where Eddie answered the door and led me into the unlit living room. His father sat in the dark close to the TV watching the pre-game activities on a screen a bit larger than the size of a postcard. He didn't say a word but recognized me with a smileless, sideward hint of a nod. I sat down on the couch.

About midway through the game the sounds of a door being

shut and some footsteps and voices came through the thin wall that separated the room with the TV from the adjacent apartment. After a few moments, loud Arabic music and singing from a record player suddenly blasted through the wall drowning out the sounds of the TV.

"Ah, b'Jesus, can you believe it!" shouted Eddie's father. He jumped from his seat and began pounding on the wall and shouting, "Turn that damn noise down!" His angry shouts had no effect. The sounds from the next apartment were so loud I doubted if the neighbors could hear the pounding and shouting. Eddie's father continued his angry yelling and banging on the wall, but still to no avail. Then in his thick Irish brogue he began ranting about "those damn foreigners next door." He grabbed his walking stick, opened the front window, leaned out, and began hitting the neighbor's window with his stick, all the while shouting, "Turn off that noise," and muttering about "damn foreigners." Then I heard the sound of breaking glass. "Ah, shit," Eddie's father yelled. "What's a person to do?" He sheepishly closed his window and turned off the TV. It was obvious the time had come for me to leave. The Arabic music and singing continued, and the next day I read in the paper that the Dodgers had won the game.

"Eddie's got a good deal in Germany," said Porky. "The Army put him in rec services so he spends most of his time training and then boxing at Army bases in Europe. When he gets out he's going to get a manager and turn pro."

Porky got busy with customers so I began looking around the room. I had seen some of the faces before, but I didn't see any of my friends. The juke box played Tony Bennett singing "Rags to Riches." I recognized Puffer Riley sitting at the end of the bar. Puffer was a few years older than me but we knew each other from the gym. I waved and walked over.

"Hey, Puffer, how you been?" I said.

"I'm doing great. I got drafted, put two years in the army, and got out six months ago. I got a job in the mail room at an insurance company in the city while I'm waiting to take the exam for the Sanitation Department. What about you?"

"Not bad," I said. "I just finished fifteen months in Alaska and got two weeks of leave. I'm in for four years and have two years left."

We sat at the bar sipping beer and talking about who was where, and what they were doing. As the crowd grew, the place got smokier and noisier.

"You're the first guy in here that I recognize," I said. "I ran into Honey Walsh and he said most of the guys are still in the service."

"Yeah, mostly," said Puffer. "A few guys like Honey were 4F, some guys had police records and got rejected, and a couple of guys who got drafted got booted out right way. That happened to Jose Diaz. You remember Jose?"

"Yeah, I sat next to him in eighth grade at St. Paul's. He taught me to smoke when I was thirteen. We used to go to his apartment after school and smoke his mother's cigarettes. I remember she smoked Phillip Morris and always had a carton of them in the apartment. Jose knew how to open a pack from the bottom, take out one cigarette and put the pack back together so it looked like it had never been touched. His mother never caught on that each of her packs had nineteen cigarettes."

"I saw Jose on Pacific Street a couple of months ago," said Puffer. "He didn't tell me what happened, but he got into some trouble during basic training and landed in the brig. Then the army gave him a Bad Conduct Discharge. You'd hardly know the guy if you saw him. I'm standing there talking to him and he's looking straight at me but like he's looking right through me."

"Jose was always getting into trouble in school," I said. "Sister Julia, the old nun who taught eighth grade would whack him with a yard stick and he would just laugh at her."

Jose's mom was a tiny thing who sat at a sewing machine in a sweat shop on Bergen Street making Corde handbags. She couldn't handle Jose and his old man didn't live with them. After elementary school Jose and I went in different directions. He was never interested in sports. I'd see him on the street sometimes, but he hung out with different guys and I lost track of him. At a neighborhood reunion that I went to in 1994, a classmate from elementary school mentioned that Jose had died. A woman walking her dog early one morning had seen a body behind some bushes in a neighborhood park and called the police. It was Jose, dead from an overdose of heroin.

"Drink up boys," said Porky, "this one's on me and I'll be having one with you." He placed two new glasses of beer in front of us and filled a shot glass with whiskey.

"Here's to our health," he said lifting the shot and belting it down.

"Puffer, did you tell him about Skeets Gallagher?" asked Porky.

"What about Skeets?" I asked.

"You won't believe this," said Puffer, "but Skeets is in a monastery. He's going to be a priest. My mother told me about it after she learned it from Mrs. Gallagher," said Puffer.

He went on to tell us that Skeets had been up on the front line in Korea during some heavy fighting. It sounded pretty bad. He saw a lot of the guys he was with get killed. Skeets got shot and was sure he would never make it out of Korea alive. He was in a bunker dug into a hillside with three other guys. They had an agreement that you didn't shit in the bunker. Skeets had to go, but when he crawled out of the bunker he got shot by a North Korean sniper. After he got shot he made a vow that if God got him out of Korea alive, Skeets would become a priest. When Skeets got discharged he kept his vow and went into a monastery in Pennsylvania.

"Skeets was lucky. Some of the guys came home in boxes," said Puffer. "Tony LaRusso got killed and Georgie King. And Red McMahon came home from Korea and got put in a VA hospital upstate. His sister told me she didn't know what was wrong with him."

Red and I had played on the same basketball team at Smith's gym. I'd known him since grade school. We were in the same class. At St. Paul's he was a choir boy and I was an altar boy. Red was a muscular kid with a mop of bright red curls. He could run faster than any kid I knew. He stuttered except when he sang in the choir at church. He had a beautiful voice and was picked to sing solos at mass. He wanted to be an altar boy but the priest put him in the choir because Red stuttered when he spoke Latin.

Red had the nicest mother. She was a meek, tiny woman who had come to the United States from Ireland to work as a housekeeper. She spoke with a soft, sing-song brogue and sprinkled her conversations with "Oh, God save us!" and "The Lord be willing!" Some days when I rang the doorbell to see if Red wanted to play ball, his mother would answer the door and then insist on sitting us at the wooden table in the kitchen and serving us hot tea. While the water heated she would ask questions and sometimes tell us about Ireland. These moments in the kitchen with Red and me were the only times I saw her full of smiles. Sometimes she would ask what we wanted to do when we grew up. Red said he wanted to row a boat across the Atlantic Ocean and visit Ireland. I told her I wanted to be a fireman and drive a hook and ladder truck like my Uncle Bob. She told me she was sure that I would become a priest.

Red's family lived in a small apartment over a grocery store and directly across the street from St. Paul's church. The only time I remember seeing Red's mother out of their apartment was at church. I never saw a visitor come to Red's apartment while I was there. Some days when Red's mother answered the apartment door, and sometimes when I saw her at church, she would be wearing sunglasses. At first I thought she wore sunglasses because she had sensitive eyes.

Red's father was a strapping, cantankerous Irishman who snarled his words with intimidating certainty and volume. Once when I was in Red's kitchen his father arrived, smelling of drink. Red and his mother froze and everything seemed to stop, like when a projector jams and the movie stops in mid-scene. Then Red and his mother—like two cats in an alley startled by the slamming of a trash can lid—looked at Red's father, waiting for his first move. He walked across the kitchen, unzipped his fly, and pissed into the sink. Some times when I was at Red's his father arrived drunk and without saying a word, walked to the bedroom, and flopped onto the bed.

Even when sober Red's father created a cowering atmosphere in the apartment. Sometimes after a report card arrived home he would ridicule Red and say he was stupid. "The trouble is you've got a thick skull," he would say. Sometimes he spoke to his wife in a way that brought fear to her face. When I saw him do these things I fantasized about being bigger and stronger and taking him on. But I knew that when Red's father arrived, it was time for me to leave.

Red's father had worked for years as a longshoreman on the Brooklyn docks but eventually drank his way out of the job. Because the family was almost destitute, the parish hired Red's father to be janitor at the school and sexton at the church. He lasted about a year and then while drunk got into a fight with the pastor, stormed out, and quit. He didn't seem to have any friends. By the time Red and I were teenagers, his father only did odd jobs like mopping floors and cleaning saloons after they closed for the night.

"Puffer, I didn't know that Red was back from Korea," I said. "I got a letter from him when I was in Alaska. He sent me a picture of him in combat gear, sitting on a wall of sandbags with a rifle across his lap. I was going to stop by and see his mother while I was home on leave."

"That poor woman's been through the meat grinder," said Puffer. "Her only son is in a V.A. hospital with who knows what. Her only daughter gets knocked up by some sailor and her father kicks her out of the house. The woman's a saint having to live with that bum of a husband."

"Drink up boys," said Porky putting two more glasses of beer in front of us. These are on Old Man Waters sitting down there at the end of the bar." I turned and looked that way. Tommy Waters lifted his glass, gave it a tilt, and sent a smile our way. Tommy was a neighborhood character and probably in his late sixties. I didn't know him well, but he knew my parents. Before he retired, Tommy worked in the subway as a motorman. Every March 17 he marched down Fifth Avenue in the St. Patrick's Day parade.

"Hey, if we stay here long enough we'll be under the table without having spent a buck between us," said Puffer.

Then Puffer suddenly pointed to the end of the bar where Tommy Waters, glass in hand and glassy eyed, stood atop the bar bantering with some customers. Porky, having a drink with a customer at the opposite end of the bar, became aware of a commotion behind him and turned. Wearing a grin and shaking his head Porky began walking Tommy's way. "He's a harmless fellow, but gets a bit off in the head after a few drinks," Porky said as he walked towards Tommy.

"Tommy, get the hell down from there before you break your neck," said Porky looking up at Tommy and joining in the laughter with others.

Tommy, ignoring Porky, shouted in his thick brogue, "I've got some words that need saying and I'll be saying them. Ladies and Gentlemen," he began. "I've got something to say to you." Between the juke box and multiple conversations and laughter going on in the crowd, Tommy had to shout and repeat his salutation several times before he got most people's attention. Someone reached behind the jukebox and lowered its volume. "It warms my heart" he said, "to see so many young Irish people down here tonight at this end of Atlantic Avenue". Lifting his glass he shouted, "And I drink to your health." A few cheers came from the crowd. "When I came to this country 50 years ago, this part of Brooklyn was filled with Irish," he went on. "They were good, hard-working people. Without them we wouldn't have subways in this city. We dug the tunnels and laid the track. But it's a pitiful sight you see when you look around the neighborhood today. Almost all the Irish are gone, disappeared, pushed out by people who don't even speak English. When the Irish came you didn't see signs in shop windows written in Gaelic. We spoke English like everyone who lives here should. Red Mike's is the only Irish business left on this street, and for how long we don't know. It's our final bastion. You go out the front door of this place and turn left and you're in San Juan. You turn right and you're in the harbor. I tell you, these Puerto Ricans, they're driving us into the sea."

By this time most of the crowd had lost interest in what Tommy had to say and had returned to their conversations. The noise level began to drown Tommy out. Someone turned the volume back up on the jukebox and Joni James began singing *Danny Boy*. Porky and two customers got Tommy back onto his bar stool.

The next morning I went to see Red's mother. The name over the doorbell that I had pressed so many times before read *Rodriquez*. I pushed the button and a young woman answered the door. A child's face peaked out from behind her. She said that she didn't know anything about who had lived in the apartment before her. She had never met them.

I never saw Red or his mother again.

CHAPTER 10

Beyond the Fallout

IN CALM SEAS TWO HOURS OUT OF San Diego, the *U.S.S. Estes* cut through the patchy, early morning coastal fog tailed by a flock of strident gulls that hovered above the stern. The crew of the *Estes* had no idea where the ship was headed. In San Diego their captain had announced they would be at sea for three months, but didn't disclose the ship's destination or mission. The Navy had classified those details as *top secret*.

As the *Estes* headed southwest my friend Moose and I leaned against the ship's rail smoking cigarettes and speculating about where we were going.

"All that meteorology equipment and the seven extra weathermen that came aboard in San Diego tell me we're headed for some remote place where there's lots of bad weather. Maybe Antarctica," said Moose.

"I hope not," I said. "I did three months in the Arctic and before that a year on Kodiak Island. I've had enough of 60 knot winds at 20 below."

Moose was 18 but didn't look old enough to be in the Navy. He was short, slender, had a peach-fuzz face and sparkling brown eyes that let you know you were dealing with a prankster. Moose grew up in a small town on the Olympic Peninsula. He loved talking about outdoor life, catching fish, hunting elk, and searching for mushrooms in the rain forest. His mom sent him packages with cookies, smoked salmon, and foods from the forest. He always shared the jerky she made from smoked cougar meat.

On the third day out of San Diego the Captain announced that the *Estes* would make a weekend stop at Pearl Harbor. While our ship was docked at Pearl Harbor Moose and I rented a car and drove around the perimeter of Oahu. On the northern coast of the island, a world-famous place for surfing, we watched 30 foot waves crash onshore. As a couple of weathermen Moose and I knew these waves had been spawned days earlier by storms thousands of miles away in the North Pacific Ocean. When our ship left Pearl Harbor, the crew manned the rail as we passed a memorial marking the place where the battle ship Arizona had been sunk by the Japanese on December 7, 1941.

Three days after we left Pearl Harbor, our ship's executive officer, a three-stripe commander, a no-nonsense, by-the-book Annapolis product, convened the crew on deck and announced our destination and mission. We were headed for Bikini, an atoll in the Marshall Islands midway between Hawaii and Australia. An atoll consists of a deep lagoon enclosed by a ring of islands strung together like beads on a necklace. Thirty-five islands surrounded Bikini's lagoon. Each island of the atoll was the sand-covered tip of a twenty-five mile coral reef that starts a mile below the ocean surface on the summit of a submerged volcano. Our executive officer disclosed that the *Estes* would serve as headquarters for a series of seventeen hydrogen bomb tests, a mission officially designated as *Operation Redwing*. We arrived at the Bikini atoll on April 15, 1956, six days after my twenty-second birthday and three weeks before the first hydrogen bomb test.

The morning after we arrived at Bikini, as the *Estes* rode lazily at anchor tethered by tons of iron chain to massive flukes buried in the floor of Bikini's lagoon, Moose and I stood on the top deck of the ship tracking a weather balloon we had just launched. The five-foot-wide helium-filled balloon carried instruments and a transmitter that radioed back weather information until the balloon burst about 60,000 feet above the surface. Beyond the reef columns of golden sunlight, like giant spotlights scanning the ocean surface, angled down through openings in the clouds. Dense, blackish-grayish curtains of rain hung from the bottoms of two towering thunderheads six miles away on the southern horizon. Off to the west the sun hid behind cottony white clouds, tingeing them with vivid reds, yellows and purples. Coconut palms swayed above the sun-bleached sand of an island 400 yards beyond our ship's bow. Conspicuously missing from the idyllic scene were any signs of the islanders who had occupied Bikini's atoll for 3000 years. Years later I learned they had been brusquely relocated to an atoll 150 miles east in 1946 when the United States Atomic Energy Commission determined that Bikini provided an ideal place to test nuclear weapons.

As Moose and I worked, we looked out on a tropical paradise. The lagoon teemed with life and the *Estes* made an ideal platform for viewing. In the ensuing days I began to realize that the beauty and exquisite adaptations of the marine life all around us existed in a violent environment of predators and victims. When I looked down into the lagoon from the ship's rail and saw flashes of glitter where sunlight caught the silvery scales on schools of fish, I could usually find a barracuda lurking nearby, poised like a giant stiletto ready to strike.

The first time I saw a flying fish, I wasn't sure what it was. I had always thought flying fish were a myth, like mermaids. Then, on the second day of our stay in the Bikini lagoon, a flying fish leaped out of the water about 100 feet from the side of the ship, leveled off about two and a half feet above the water, and traveled a good 40 feet over the surface before plunging back into the lagoon. After that I saw flying fish every day. When they leaped from the water, if I listened carefully, I could hear the buzzing sounds of their furiously beating pectoral fins propelling them through the air as they tried to outdistance the jaws of predator fish that pursued them beneath the surface. I watched albatrosses and petrels patrolling the lagoon, flying without flapping their wings, effortlessly skimming the troughs and crests of the swells, their long bills snagging fish that came close to the surface. Sometimes when the bird landed on the water with its catch, a large piratical bird dove from the sky and stole its fish; once I saw a giant sea turtle appear and drag the bird and fish back into the depths.

Every morning a group of nuclear physicists and military brass came to the weather office for a briefing given by a Navy officer who was a meteorologist. The scientists' main interest was the forecast for the winds aloft and the projected path of the radioactive cloud that would be created on Friday, May 4, when the first hydrogen bomb was tested. Nothing was mentioned about the monumental disaster that had taken place here two years before, following the detonation of *Bravo*, a hydrogen bomb with a destructive force of 1,000 Hiroshima-size bombs. Except for some information I learned from T. S. Jones, one of the ship's cooks, I didn't know anything about the *Bravo* disaster until years after I had left the Navy.

T.S. Jones was the only crew member I knew who had been aboard the *Estes* at the time of *Bravo*. T.S. worked in the kitchen of the enlisted men's mess hall. He had been in the Navy for fourteen years and twice had reached the rank of second class petty officer, only to be demoted back to third class because of drunken brawls he had gotten into while on shore leave.

T.S. had seen me launching weather balloons and one day while several of us were showering, he asked me if I could get him a balloon. He wanted a weather balloon for his girlfriend's eight-year-old son in San Diego. I couldn't imagine what a kid would do with a weather balloon. It was too large to inflate by mouth and in any case would be more than an eight-year-old could safely handle. But T.S. and I made a deal anyway. He would sneak me two lemon meringue pies from the ship's commissary and I would get him a balloon.

In the Navy, back then, getting a tattoo anywhere that showed when you were in military dress was an offense for which you could be given a bad conduct discharge or put in the brig; if you had a tattoo on your neck you were history. But when you were in the shower you saw guys with tattoos all over the hidden parts of their bodies. You couldn't predict who would have tattoos; some spit-and-polish types turned out to have huge American flags tattooed across their backs, while some grubby rough-and-tumble sailors had nothing. Seen in the shower T.S.'s body was a billboard advertising the imagination and artistic skills found in the tattoo parlors of Hong Kong and Bangkok. His collection included a blue, five-inch propeller on each buttock and a domestic house fly on the tip of his penis.

When I arrived at Bikini I knew nothing about the previous nuclear tests except that they had been going on in the area since 1946. I learned from T.S. that during the 1954 tests a wind shift resulted in radioactive fallout from *Bravo*'s cloud contaminating the crew of a Japanese tuna boat operating about 100 miles east of Bikini. T.S. said all of the crew got sick from radiation and that one of them died.

I've since learned something about atomic and hydrogen bombs and how they release energy in the form of heat and deadly radiation. Atomic bombs work on the principle of splitting atoms, while hydrogen bombs work on an opposite principle—the fusion of atoms. When uranium atoms are split during the explosion of an atomic bomb, the temperature in the core of the explosion exceeds one million degrees, the same temperature as on the surface of the sun. The fusion of hydrogen atoms in a hydrogen bomb requires temperatures in the range of one million degrees. This is achieved by using an atomic bomb as the detonator for the hydrogen bomb.

When uranium atoms are split and hydrogen atoms are fused during the detonation of a nuclear weapon, energy is released that had sat latent within those atoms since they were formed at the time of the *Big Bang*. The release of deadly radiation from atoms during a nuclear explosion mimics the tale in Arabian mythology where fire sets free imprisoned evil genies who are invisible to humans and who travel the world to plague mankind.

In 2005 when I began researching the nuclear weapons tests at Bikini I learned from documents declassified by Congress during the 1980s and 1990s that on February 28, 1954, the day before the *Bravo* test, high altitude winds over Bikini had shifted from a northerly to a northeasterly flow, a worrisome development because several islands east of the test site were inhabited. Analyses, calculations and discussions only 6 hours before detonation led to the decision to proceed with the test. *Bravo*'s huge explosion vaporized one of the 35 islands of the Bikini atoll and produced a crater in the coral reef more than a mile wide and 1000 feet deep.

I learned from printed testimony given by eyewitnesses that just before dawn on March 1, 1954, native fishermen on the beach at Rongelap, 100 miles east of Bikini, were startled by a brilliant light in the western sky. About eight minutes later they heard an enormous boom and felt a blast of warm air rush over the island. They were terrified and had no idea what was happening. Minutes later they saw the sun rise in the east. Some of the Rongelap natives interviewed described March 1, 1954, as the day the sun rose twice.

During the hours that followed the detonation of *Bravo,* the upper-level winds over Bikini had assumed an easterly flow, moving the huge radioactive cloud towards the atolls at Rongelap and Utrik, homes to 236 islanders. Six hours after the blast, the natives on Rongelap saw fine, grayish-white powder—the minute residue of incinerated coral reef—falling from the sky. It stuck to their skin, hair and clothing. When it stopped falling three hours later, everything on the island—the coconut palms, thatched roofs, outrigger canoes, sandy beaches—were covered with an inch of radioactive powder. Some children who had never seen the real thing thought it was snow and played in it.

Within hours the islanders developed itchy skin, nausea, vomiting, and diarrhea. Within days they began to experience skin burns, eye pain, and hair loss. It would be months and years before they saw the malignant consequences of the mayhem that was inflicted on their DNA. The contaminated air contained radioactive strontium and iodine that entered their lungs, moved into their blood streams, and disseminated throughout their bodies. The radioactive strontium deposited in their bones and teeth, and for decades emitted radiation that damaged bone marrow cells, caused mutations, and predisposed the islanders to develop leukemia.

The radioactive iodine they inhaled concentrated in their thyroid glands, destroyed cells, caused mutations, and resulted in hypothyroidism and thyroid cancer. Native babies, their thyroids injured by radiation while they were still fetuses, were born with severe deformities. Those who survived into childhood suffered from impaired growth and mental retardation if not worse, and some of them also developed thyroid cancer.

Some Rongelap women who became pregnant after being contaminated with fallout—in some cases years after being contaminated—were horrified when they went into labor and instead of a baby, delivered a soft-ball-sized mass of tissue that contained hundreds of tiny fluid-filled cysts. These malformations resulted from the fertilization of radiation-damaged eggs that grew into a mass of cystic placental tissue lacking a fetus.

The islanders reported that the day after the *Bravo* detonation a military seaplane arrived at Rongelap and two men with Geiger counters spent about twenty minutes taking readings of rain water catchments and soil. They warned the islanders not to drink the water and then departed. Fifty hours after being contaminated with radioactive fallout, the inhabitants of Rongelap were finally evacuated. Those on Utrik, 300 miles east of Bikini, were not evacuated for 72 hours. Until all these natives were evacuated and decontamination measures were initiated, radiation from the clothing they wore, the ground they slept on, the food they ate, the air they breathed, continued to inflict injury.

The failure to evacuate the islanders prior to detonation of *Bravo*, as had been done with other native islanders before previous tests, remains unexplained. The delay in evacuating the natives once contamination had occurred has also never been accounted for. Within days of the *Bravo* disaster, the United States Atomic Energy Commission stated that the contamination resulted from a last-minute shift in wind direction. Documents released in 1994 under the Freedom of Information Act revealed that the wind had begun to shift 12 hours before the detonation and that the military people directing the test were aware of this. Whether the *Bravo* disaster resulted from human error, misjudgment, chicanery, or some combination, has never been resolved to the satisfaction of Marshall Islanders. In some of the 1994 testimony given to Congress by government officials from the Marshall Islands, the officials state plainly and with some outrage that they were used as guinea pigs. The failure to cancel the test when the winds shifted, the delay in evacuating natives once contamination had occurred, and the revelation that before the tests began the Atomic Energy Commission had put in place a detailed plan to study the effects of radiation exposure on humans all supported the Marshall Islanders' contention.

On May 4, 1956, the day of the first hydrogen bomb test of *Operation Redwing*, I witnessed the detonation of a bomb that had a destructive force about three times greater than the bomb dropped on Hiroshima. Just before dawn that morning I sat on the deck of the *Estes* with my back to ground zero which was about twenty miles away. With my safety goggles in place I couldn't see anything—it was like being blind. I sat wondering what it would be like when the bomb exploded. We had been told that we wouldn't see or feel anything. When the bomb exploded I heard a tremendous boom that seemed to shake the atmosphere. When the all-clear was given I moved to the ship's rail, and even with my goggles still on I saw an enormous, towering fireball climbing in the sky. As I watched the cloud I began to imagine horrific scenes of cities obliterated and people incinerated.

Lingering radioactivity from all the tests contaminated the environment at Bikini. This meant that all of us were exposed to radiation, not only during the tests, but during the lulls between tests. When Moose and I were off duty we sometimes fished from the ship's stern where posted signs warned not to eat the fish because they were radioactive. Some days the captain gave permission for the crew to swim from the ship at anchor in the lagoon. I was among the hearty who jumped from the side of the ship; the less adventuresome descended the ship's ladder to reach the water. As I leaped from the ship's deck pinching my nose closed, I remembered summer days as a teenager jumping into New York harbor from barges moored along the Brooklyn waterfront. While we swam, four members of the deck force, armed with M1 rifles, stood guard along the ship's rail in case a shark was spotted. A shark never showed up but I later wondered about the wisdom of shooting one had it appeared since a wounded shark might attract other sharks—not to mention the wisdom of swimming in water contaminated with radioactivity. I had no qualms about swimming in the lagoon because if the Navy said we could swim, I thought it must be safe.

Some afternoons we rode our ship's water taxi to an island where the Navy had built a softball field. Signs posted on the island warned not to eat the coconuts because they were radioactive. The Navy supplied cold cans of Schlitz, two per sailor. One afternoon after a hydrogen bomb test had taken place in the morning, our ship's team was playing softball on the island against a team from another ship. Midway through the game, Moose, our team's shortstop, called timeout. "Something's wrong," he said. "I just noticed my radiation badge is pink. It was blue when we left the ship." Everyone began checking their radiation badges and found they were pink, the sign of radiation exposure. "There's something's hot around here," a sailor yelled. "I've played three games on this island in the past two weeks and my badge never changed from blue." Just then the fog horn on the *Estes* blasted the general alarm, a signal for us to return to the ship. We grabbed our gear and ran towards the lagoon where we saw the water taxi headed for us. From the water taxi's radio we learned that a wind shift had caused our area to experience heavy radioactive fallout. When we reached the *Estes* we hustled below deck, all portholes and hatches were sealed, the anchor was hauled, and as we motored out of the area we began decontamination procedures. Topside, members of the deck crew wearing special clothing hosed down the ship's surfaces; below deck we stripped, showered, and sent our contaminated clothing to the ship's laundry.

After 17 hydrogen bomb detonations the tests ended. The atomic scientists returned to their laboratories in California and New Mexico, and the naval ships hauled anchors and moved away. Two days before the *Estes* departed Bikini for San Diego, I noticed a new ship anchored near us in the lagoon. On its hull were the words "*Scripps Institute of Oceanography, San Diego.*" I learned that the ship carried a team of biologists and oceanographers who had come to assess the environmental impact of the nuclear tests.

Had they come to Bikini ten years earlier, they would have seen families living in the traditions of their ancestors. They would have seen people gathering coconuts, papaya, taro, and turtle eggs from the land. They would have seen natives in hand-made outrigger canoes harvesting fish, crustaceans, and other marine life from the lagoon, and sailing hand-made rigs between the islands to trade goods and visit relatives. Instead they saw a fleet of military vessels riding at anchor in the lagoon and islands that were completely deserted.

The scientists from Scripps had been here after nuclear tests in previous years. They already knew many of the harrowing secrets hidden in the idyllic scene, about radioactivity that permeated the vegetation on the island and the food chains in the lagoon. They knew that the radioactivity would persist for centuries, making Bikini uninhabitable and banishing its natives to lives as refugees. If they didn't know it when they arrived, they would soon learn that the distortions in the ocean current where it passed over the submerged reef near their anchorage marked the place where an island had sat for millions of years until it was vaporized two months ago by a hydrogen bomb.

Years later, while I was a faculty member at Washington University School of Medicine, I learned about the *St. Louis Baby Tooth Survey* conducted from 1959 to 1970. Concerned about world-wide radioactive fallout from nuclear weapon tests, investigators at Washington University organized a community effort that collected 85,000 baby teeth and measured their radioactive strontium content. They found that the radioactive strontium in baby teeth of children born from 1945 to 1965 increased by 100-fold and that the levels of radioactive strontium rose and fell in correlation with the testing of nuclear bombs.

The code names chosen by the military for the overall operation and for each of the hydrogen bombs had a connection to Native Americans, a feature that lacked sensitivity to say the least. *Redwing* was a famous chief of a northern plains Sioux tribe whose land was stolen by the United States government. Sixteen of the seventeen hydrogen bombs were assigned the name of a Native American tribe. A hydrogen bomb 300 times more powerful than the bomb dropped on Hiroshima was designated *Cherokee*, an ironic label considering that the removal of natives from Bikini in 1945 by the United States government mirrored the government's forced migration of the *Cherokees* from Tennessee and Georgia to Oklahoma in 1838 on the *Trail of Tears*.

While *Lacrosse*, the first test of *Operation Redwing* went as we had been told it would, some of the other nuclear tests I observed were plagued by adversity, as the *Bravo* test had been in 1954, and, as with *Bravo*, information about those problems was classified by the military as *top secret*. Decades passed before members of Congress learned about many of the inhumane and disastrous events that occurred at Bikini during the nuclear tests. Midway through the 1956 tests, half of our radiation-detection badges were discovered to be defective. This meant that our exposure to radiation could only be estimated. The crew was never told about the badges or estimated radiation levels, and the information remained secret until it was declassified thirty years later. In one of the tests I witnessed, a B52 six miles above Bikini released *Cherokee*, a hydrogen bomb that missed its target by four miles, another fact that remained secret for decades. Following the detonation of Navajo—a surface explosion I witnessed from the ship—a wind shift resulted in heavy radioactive fallout showering one of the islands occupied by U.S. Air Force personnel. Some of them developed leukemia.

To the crew of the *Estes* secrecy dominated *Operation Redwing*. At the outset they didn't know where they were going or what they would be doing once they arrived. Then they spent three months at Bikini but were never told about their defective radiation dosimeters or the amount of radiation exposure they received. Decades passed before they learned about the errors and disastrous events that took place during the tests. Today, fifty years after the nuclear weapons tests at Bikini secrets remain. We still don't know the health status of the thousands of military personnel who were exposed to radiation during the tests.

CHAPTER 11

Bones

Sailors hungry for Sunday lunch lined the passageway leading into the enlisted-men's mess, a spacious compartment in the ship's bowels. Three times a day I and 400 of my fellow crew members came here to eat at long steel tables bolted to the deck. Today, each of us checked to see if our seven-digit military I.D. number appeared on a list posted outside of the mess hall. The numbers identified those of us assigned to be official observers of tomorrow morning's hydrogen bomb test.

When our ship, the *U.S.S. Estes*, sailed from San Diego three weeks before, our captain had announced we were on a special mission, but gave no particulars. Midway across the Pacific Ocean he informed the crew that the *Estes* would serve as the command ship for *Operation Redwing*, the 1956 nuclear weapons tests at Bikini, an atoll midway between Hawaii and Australia.

When I got through the chow line I spied Willie at one of the tables.

"Hey, Willie," I said, setting down my tray and taking the seat next to him. "You on the list?"

"Yeah, what about you?"

"Makes it two in a row," I answered.

Willie grew up near Seminole, Oklahoma. Like me he had

been in the Navy for almost four years. He had the wiry frame of a long-distance runner. Ruddy skin hugged the bones of his face. Barely twenty-two, Willie already had a touch of the gritty, weathered look of a Marlboro Man. Willie and I belonged to the ship's ten-member meteorology unit. Sometimes, during a lull in the work, we would talk about life before the Navy—about girls, sports, and where we grew up. He would tell me about small-town Oklahoma, about seeing tornadoes move across the open country, about hailstones the size of golf balls pelting cattle that had no place to hide, about Friday nights in the summer when the rodeo came to town and, after a few beers, some locals would leave the stands to compete in the amateur bull-riding contest.

I would tell him about sizzling summer days when my buddies and I dove naked into New York harbor from barges moored to piers at the foot of Amity Street, about hanging from the back of the Ocean Avenue trolley headed for Coney Island, about playing ball on busy, asphalt streets using a broomstick to whack a pink rubber ball you could buy for a dime at the corner newsstand. Willie's dream was to go to New York some day and see his Oklahoma idol, Mickey Mantle, play center field in Yankee Stadium.

Sometimes we talked about life after the Navy. He couldn't wait to get back to Oklahoma. He had a girlfriend there. They would get married as soon as he got home. Then he'd go to work in the oil fields.

"My father works on the rigs and can get me in," he said. "It's the best job you can get around Seminole. It pays real good."

I told Willie that I had gotten interested in science at the Navy Weather School and that when my four years were up I wanted to go to college and become a scientist. I told him I had gotten a high school equivalency diploma through the Navy and hoped that would be good enough to get me in somewhere.

Willie and I often worked the same eight-hour shifts preparing maps with the latest weather information radioed from land stations and ships all over the Northern Pacific Ocean. Our job was to decode the information and enter it onto a map the size of a large beach towel. Every six hours members of the meteorology team prepared new weather maps of the Pacific Ocean north of the Equator. When Willie and I did a map we took turns, one decoding and reading aloud, the other listening and with a fine-tipped pen writing the information on the map at the latitude and longitude of the reporting station. In a space about the size of a quarter, we entered symbols and numbers depicting the atmospheric pressure, temperature, dew point, cloud cover, direction and force of the wind and a remarkable amount—considering the small space—of other meteorological data. When we completed plotting the information on the map, we had entered more than one hundred quarter-sized clusters of markings.

When we finished each map, a commissioned officer who was an expert meteorologist took over to analyze the map and prepare the immediate weather forecast. He worked fast. He knew that before he was finished military brass and nuclear physicists would be looking over his shoulder and asking questions. Weather conditions, especially the winds aloft, were critical determinants in the decision to proceed with, or delay, a nuclear test.

As Willie and I chomped on bologna sausage sandwiches—for some reason the Navy always called bologna "bologna sausage"—the crowded mess hall echoed with sounds: the clanking of soiled trays, silverware, and racks of glasses as they rumbled along a conveyor belt that disappeared through a slot in a bulkhead; the shouting of cooks back in the kitchen and commissary workers on the food line; the buzzing of a roomful of sailors all talking at the same time. Except for the engine room, the mess hall at meal times was the noisiest place on the ship. It was the clearing house for ship gossip.

"You see those civilians who came aboard this morning?" Willie asked.

"Yeah, I got a look at them. Some of them looked pretty old," I said.

"Chief Butcher gave us the scoop on them," said a sailor sitting near the end of the table. "They're congressmen and journalists. One of them is Bob Considine. You remember the movie *Thirty Seconds Over Tokyo*? He's the guy who wrote the book."

"Ain't that just like the Navy," said Frankie, a burly Louisiana Cajun who played third base on our softball team and worked in the ship's print shop. "They tell us we can't write anything in our letters about where we are and what's happening here. We can't seal our letters cause they gotta get censored, and then they bring out a bunch of reporters for tomorrow's blast. Figure that one!"

"I made the list," Frankie went on. "First time for me. What's it like?"

"You don't see anything when it goes off," said another sailor. "You got on these black, wrap-around goggles that make you look like an alien. They cover half your face. You can't see zip with 'em on."

"First you hear the blast, then you feel some heat. Then they tell you to keep your goggles on but it's OK to turn around and look. You see this unbelievable fireball mushrooming way the hell up there," said Willie.

***

The next morning I arrived topside as the faint glow of first light started its climb on the eastern horizon, bleaching the night's darkness, beginning to silhouette the distant cumulonimbus clouds. A barely perceptible breeze wandered about the deck. The ship's generators hummed in the background. Lights on vessels anchored nearby speckled the surrounding darkness.

I made my way along the deck until I came to the spot I had been assigned, then slowly eased my haunches down onto the steel deck. A ship's quartermaster came along, passing out safety goggles. A lieutenant gave last minute instructions: "Be sure your radiation badge is attached to your belt," he barked. I reached down and felt mine in place. "Make sure your goggles don't let any light in," he went on. "Everything should be totally black. If you're seeing any light, you could be permanently blinded when the bomb explodes." With the goggles on I opened my eyes as wide as I could and thought, "This must be what it's like to be blind." I felt vulnerable. "Take your safety position," the lieutenant shouted. I assumed the safety position: butt and soles on the deck, goggles tightly secured, back to ground zero, face buried in the bend of my elbow, elbow tucked between flexed knees.

Then for ten minutes, I sat in total darkness, the silence broken only by fragments of conversation that crackled from the ship's loudspeakers as the Command Center on our ship and the pilot of the B52 confirmed the last minute details of altitude, winds, target coordinates, bomb release, and post-detonation maneuvers. As the countdown reached the final minutes, I felt my uneasiness grow. Up in the belly of the B52 sat a hydrogen bomb 300 times more powerful than the bomb dropped on Hiroshima.

The voice on the loudspeaker reeled off the final count. "5 - 4 - 3 - 2 - 1 - Detonation!" In two seconds I heard a colossal boom and felt the strong sensation of heat on my back, as if an oven door had been opened right behind me. Then, even with my eyes closed and covered with goggles and with my face buried in my elbow, I saw something: a vivid, brilliant, yellow-orange light that surrounded my vision like a panoramic outdoor movie screen. There were two odd grayish spots, like oblong shadows, angling across the uniform brightness.

I panicked. "How can I be seeing something? I've got on these goggles. The blast is 15 miles behind me. Something's wrong!" The image was unlike anything I had ever seen. It lasted for only a few seconds, long enough to imprint in my memory. Then it faded. My heart raced. Certain this was doomsday, I braced expecting a finale, wondering if I would feel it or just be gone. Scenarios flew across my mind. "Maybe a chain reaction made the blast bigger than predicted. Maybe a navigation error put our ship too close to Ground Zero. Maybe the B52 missed its target and dropped the bomb near our ship."

I waited, frozen in fear. The sober voice on the loudspeaker said, "Maintain your safety positions!" My panic began to ease as I realized that whatever had gone wrong, we had survived, at least for the moment. Then the voice announced, "It is safe to sit up, but do not remove your goggles or look towards ground zero." Another minute passed and again the voice sounded, "It is now safe to turn around, but do not—I repeat—do not remove your goggles."

I turned and saw, even though I was still wearing those total blackout goggles, an enormous, mushroom-shaped fireball, its top well above 100,000 feet high and growing. The gargantuan intruder in the early morning sky defied imagination. "Holy Shit!" a nearby voice yelled. Gradually the intensity of the fireball diminished and the incredible scene began to fade, like the lights in a theatre at the start of a play. Then, total blackness returned. After several minutes came the announcement, "It is safe to remove your goggles." When I lifted my goggles I was instantly blinded. It was like looking directly at the sun. When my eyes adjusted I moved to the ship's rail. I stood frozen, watching a fireball four miles wide climb in the sky. The fireball sat on top of a gray cylindrical column that glowed at its core and reached to the ground. This surreal scene was backlit by the growing light of dawn on the horizon.

Then from the loudspeaker came the command, "Prepare to take seas broadside!" The ship began to roll from side to side as a tsunami-like wave created by the atmospheric shock from the detonation reached us. The ship's movement threw me backwards but I grabbed the railing before I fell. I felt my heart pounding. The heaving of the ship continued as a series of huge sea swells reached it.

"Jesus Christ," a sailor cried. "Are we gonna flip?"

After a few tense moments, the swells diminished and the heaving passed. The crew held fast to the rail, fixated on the cloud. An uneasy silence set in. Even later, after we had dispersed and returned to our regular duties, nobody talked about the morning's events.

The next day our ship motored to ground zero. As we slowly circled the site, hundreds of sailors stood on deck, gazing in silence like mourners at a graveside when the casket is lowered. Where an island had been for millions of years, all that remained were distortions in the water where the ocean current flowed over a decapitated coral reef. Gone were the sand, the palms, the coconuts, the birds, the sea shells—all vaporized in an instant by one million degrees Fahrenheit.

After I left the Navy and started college, I sometimes experienced flashbacks where I saw the strange yellow-orange image with grayish shadows that I saw that day at Bikini. Today I can close my eyes and still see it. When I was a first-year medical student studying anatomy I looked at an X-ray of an arm and realized that the odd grayish shadows in the image I saw that morning at Bikini, were my radius and ulna, the bones in my arm.

Four years ago I began to research the 1956 nuclear tests at Bikini. I found information that had been classified as secret until Congress made it public in 1992. I spoke with some former shipmates. I learned that half of the radiation dosimeter badges we wore at Bikini were defective. I learned that sailors who had been assigned to certain groups never had safety goggles while sailors assigned to other groups always had them. I learned that many crew members saw the bones in their arms. I learned that after one test military personnel on one of the islands were showered with heavy fallout and some of them later developed leukemia. I learned that the mushroom cap of the hydrogen bomb they exploded the day I saw my bones penetrated the stratosphere, then detached from its stem and expanded, eventually covering an area of about 7,000 square miles, roughly the size of the State of New Jersey. I learned that it circumnavigated the globe for years sprinkling radioactive strontium everywhere it went, strontium that ended up in the growing bones and teeth of children in every country north of the Equator. I learned that the journalists had been invited that day because it was the first time a hydrogen bomb got dropped from a B52, and that the government wanted the Russians and Chinese to know we had the capability to deliver a hydrogen bomb anywhere on the globe. I learned that the bomb they dropped that day missed its target by four miles.

None of my sources said whether it was four miles closer to us than it was supposed to be, or four miles further away.

CHAPTER 12

Tan-Man

R OGERS STOOD ABOUT TWENTY FEET AWAY, slapping gray paint onto the ship's railing and shooting glances down at the helicopter deck.

"Hey, do you see that fella down there?" he yelled.

"Yeah, he's down there like that for a bit most afternoons," I said, continuing to track the weather balloon I'd just launched.

Rogers was a crew member who in seaman's jargon was known as a *deck ape*. He spent most of his days doing ship's maintenance —scrubbing, polishing, chipping old paint off, putting new paint on.

"That boy's either a nut case or he's got a lot of clout," said Rogers continuing to paint between quick peeks at the scene below.

Spread-eagle on the helicopter deck—and totally naked—lay a short, fit man, probably in his late fifties, with wavy, shoulder-length gray hair, a trim white beard, and a world-class, shadowless tan.

"The first time I saw him was about two weeks ago." I said. "I had to do a double take. He was out there just like today, bare-assed on a towel, working on his tan."

The *U.S.S. Estes* rode lazily at anchor in the calm, turquoise waters of the lagoon at Bikini, an atoll in the Marshall Islands midway between Hawaii and Australia. The *Estes* housed the command center of *Operation Redwing*, a series of 17 hydrogen bomb tests conducted in the Marshall Islands in 1956. My journey to Bikini began when I quit high school in 1952, enlisted in the Navy for four years, got trained in meteorology, and after tours of duty on Kodiak Island, Alaska, and in the Canadian Arctic, was assigned to the Estes.

"That fella's gonna get cooked, lying out there like that," said Rogers. "He is one strange cookie."

"I'm sure he's one of the scientists," I said, continuing to track the weather balloon. "He comes to some of the daily weather briefings. Never says much but when he speaks, it's with a German accent. He's gotta be a scientist; they're the only guys who walk around the ship in shorts, tee shirts and sandals."

Rogers continued to paint, then looked my way and asked, "Why do you guys keep sending up those balloons?"

"They tell us about the winds and weather upstairs," I said. "There's an instrument pack and a radio transmitter attached to the balloon. The radio sends back information until the balloon pops when it gets up about ten miles. The scientists use the information to predict where the mushroom cloud and the radioactivity will go."

Lowering his voice, Rogers stopped painting and said, "I tell ya something, I don't like all this radioactivity stuff. You can't see it or feel it, but you know it's all over the place. The sign on the ship's stern says it's o.k. to fish, but don't eat what you catch because it's radioactive. Then over on the islands the signs say, 'Don't eat the cocoanuts, they're radioactive.' Last week I played in a softball game over on one of the islands and saw coconuts that were shaped like bananas from the radiation.

"Yeah, I know what you mean," I said, " but the Navy checks our badges every week, so they ought to know if we're getting exposed."

"Yeah, but will they'll tell us? You know the Navy; we might get a letter ten years from now saying we got exposed."

"You think if they knew we're getting zapped, they wouldn't tell us?"

"Maybe they would," he answered, "but from what I hear, once you get zapped, you can't get unzapped."

Rogers began to move his paint bucket and drop cloth, then stopped and said, "Hey, look, Tan-Man just put on a robe and he's climbing down from the flight deck."

In the days prior to each test, Tan-Man and the other scientists left the ship by helicopter early each morning and returned to the ship later in the day. On the day of a test, they all remained on board the Estes where they controlled the test from the command center. One morning during the countdown to detonation of a 3.5 megaton hydrogen bomb, a situation developed that solved the mystery of Tan-Man.

On that morning, on one of the islands, a hydrogen bomb with a potential destructive force equal to 200 Hiroshima bombs sat inside of a corrugated metal shack atop a 300-foot high steel structure similar to a forest fire lookout tower. I had been assigned to be an official observer of the test—government policy required that crew members serve as official observers of each detonation. I arrived topside before dawn and after finding my station, eased down into a sitting position on the hard deck. It never crossed my mind that observer might be a code word for experimental subject or guinea pig. This was 1956—the era of skepticism about government intentions and pronouncements lay a decade in the future. My only fear during that summer came from persistent rumors that the Brooklyn Dodgers might move to Los Angeles.

A ship's quartermaster distributed safety goggles while a Lieutenant recited the safety procedures. A voice on the ship's loudspeakers announced, "We are at T-minus 30 minutes and counting." A barely perceptible breeze wandered about the deck. Ship's generators hummed in the background. Lights on nearby vessels speckled the surrounding darkness. Sporadically, a crackle of static came from the ship's loudspeakers. Fifteen miles across the lagoon sat Ground Zero.

As the countdown proceeded, the faint glow of first light started its climb on the eastern horizon, bleaching the night's darkness, silhouetting the distant clouds. From the loudspeakers came, "T-minus 20 minutes and counting." I assumed the safety position and adjusted my goggles. Having witnessed other detonations, I knew the routine—goggles strapped on tight; butt on the deck; back to Ground Zero; face in elbow; and elbow between knees. Then came the announcement: "The countdown is on hold. We are at T-minus 15 and holding." Pauses during countdowns were uncommon and usually brief. After several minutes of silence the voice from the loudspeaker advised , "We are holding at T-minus 15."

Several more minutes of silence passed. Then the loudspeakers blared, "Abort the test! Abort the test! Prepare to launch chopper." Leaving my safety position, I moved to the ship's railing and looked towards the flight deck. The blades of the helicopter were already rotating, the revving and backfiring of its engines almost drowning out the voices around me.

Then I spied him. In shorts, t-shirt and floppy sandals, he hurried aft, rushing as if late for an appointment, his long hair bouncing in synch with his steps. When he reached the flight deck ladder, he grabbed both handrails and bounded up the steps. Without hesitating, he hopped into the chopper cockpit and fastened his harness. With the finesse of a raptor leaving its perch, the helicopter became airborne and headed to its target, the island with the bomb. When the chopper returned in 20 minutes without Tan-Man, and the ship's crew was ordered to go below deck and seal all hatches, I realized why the long-haired man with the fabulous tan had come to Bikini.

Although he was 15 miles away, in my mind's eye I could see him as he stepped down onto the beach from the chopper, shielded his eyes from the sand raised by the downdraft of rotating blades, crouched as he scurried away from the noise and turbulence, brushed sand from his beard and disheveled hair, waved the pilot a silent *auf wie-*

dershehen, then watched the chopper lift off. I imagined him alone on the beach, walking towards the tower, the silence broken only by the crunchy cadence of sandals on sand.

I wondered what he thought about while he climbed the tower's 300 steps, breathing deeper as he rose, then paused at the top, entered the shack, and began to manually disarm a live hydrogen bomb. I wondered what thoughts he had while he worked only one misstep away from becoming vaporized atoms of carbon, nitrogen, oxygen and a few salts, riding to the top of a mushroom cloud.

Later I learned more about the day's events. In 1956 the technology that controlled the detonation of hydrogen bombs was primitive. During the countdown, radio signals transmitted from the ship controlled the steps in the process that led to activation and finally detonation of the bomb. Once the process was initiated, after a certain point in the countdown, the bomb could not be disarmed by a radio signal from a remote location. On the day of the aborted test, an undisclosed problem had arisen after passing that *point of no return* in the countdown, creating a situation where a live hydrogen bomb sat atop the tower and had to be manually disarmed.

After that day rumors spread that Tan-Man was a nuclear physicist who came to the United States from Germany after World War II, worked in one of the Department of Defense Atomic Laboratories, and was an expert at assembling and disabling nuclear bombs. The afternoon of the aborted test, as I tracked another weather balloon from the top deck of the ship, I looked down at the helicopter pad and saw that he was back, working on his tan.

CHAPTER 13

Periodic Reminders

JUST BEFORE DAWN ON A MAY MORNING in 1956, I sat in silence with shipmates on the deck of the *U.S.S. Estes* looking into the black nothingness behind the safety goggles that covered my eyes. I listened to the final instructions that blared from the ship's loudspeakers and wondered what it would feel like in a few moments when a hydrogen bomb 300 times greater than the Hiroshima bomb exploded 15 miles behind me.

The *U.S.S. Estes* was command ship for *Operation Redwing*, a series of 17 hydrogen bomb tests conducted at Bikini and Enewetak, atolls in the Marshall Islands midway between Hawaii and Australia. I sat with my back to ground zero, my goggles tightly strapped over my face, my face buried in the bend of my elbow, and my elbow tucked between my knees. From the loudspeakers a voice with the exactness of a metronome ticked off the final seconds of the countdown. Then I heard a colossal blast and felt a strong sensation of heat on my back, as if a furnace door had been opened right behind me. Even with my eyes closed and covered with goggles and my face buried in my elbow, I saw something: a brilliant, yellow-orange panoramic image that contained two oblong, gray shadows. The image was unlike anything I'd ever seen. The ship's crew had been told that as long as we had our goggles on correctly we wouldn't see anything when the bomb exploded. I panicked when I saw the light through my goggles, certain it was doomsday. I braced, expecting a finale, wondering if I would feel it, or just be gone. I had no idea what the image was, but six years later, as a first year medical student, I looked at an x-ray of an arm and realized that the oblong, grayish shadows were my radius and ulna, the bones in my arm.

Twenty years later, when I was 42, a common malady of middle age resurrected my memory of that day when I saw the bones in my arm. Not that I had forgotten. Every detail had been hardwired into my frontal lobes that morning at Bikini. The malady of middle age intruded during the last minutes of a presentation I was giving to medical students about the pathology of cancer. I had spent the first 45 minutes of the class demonstrating the salient features of cancer using a series of photographs projected onto a screen at the front of the auditorium. As I finished discussing the final photograph, I glanced down at my lecture outline to check that I had not left out any important points. That's when I panicked. I couldn't read a word of the outline. Everything was out of focus. I squinted, took a step back, bent the 25-watt gooseneck lectern lamp closer to my outline, but nothing I did brought the words into focus. Then I looked up and saw 150 faces looking at me wearing puzzled expressions that ranged from "Are we finished?'" to "Is he all right?" I ended the class trusting that I had covered everything I had intended to.

For several months before, whenever my wife Nancy saw me holding an article at arms' length while I read it, she would say, "You need to make an appointment to get eyeglasses." She was right, but being busy and able to get by as long as I read in bright light and didn't get too close to the page, I had procrastinated. The incident during the cancer lecture forced taking action. I made an appointment to see Mort Smith, a close friend and faculty colleague, and a Professor of Ophthalmology at Washington University in St. Louis.

★★★

Two weeks later, I sat alone in an examination room in the Eye Clinic and heard footsteps in the hallway getting closer. I looked up just as Mort entered the room wearing a friendly smile.

"Sounds like it's time for your first pair of glasses," he said. "Welcome to middle age."

"Since this is your first eye exam I'll need to dilate your pupils, check for glaucoma, take some baseline measurements, and get good looks at each retina. Then I'll determine how much correction to put into your glasses."

He dimmed the room lights and as he began the retinal exam, he said: "Look straight ahead. Try not to move your eyes, I want to get a good look at each retina." He pointed the bright beam into my left eye and moved it around while looking through a large glass lens. "Try to keep looking straight ahead."

After a minute he moved the bright light to my right eye, took a long look and then went back to the left eye. Then back again to the right eye.

"Sorry this is taking so long, I just need to look around a bit more." He switched again to the left eye.

Then I heard the soft, "*Hmmm.*"

Sliding his stool away, he stood up, stepped back and looked directly at me, his face wearing a ponderous expression. As he spoke, I detected the slight shift in register. "I'd like to have Frank Edwards take a look," Mort said. "I'm seeing something in your right retina that I want his opinion on. Frank's new here, a Hopkins-trained neuro-ophthalmologist. His office is right down the hall. Be back in a minute."

"A neuro-ophthalmologist, that's a pretty specialized guy", I thought. I began to feel a bit uneasy wondering what Mort had seen.

Mort returned, introductions were exchanged, then Edwards sat down at the oculoscope. He didn't look very long before turning towards Mort. "Yeah, that's what it is."

"Richard, I think we may have a problem here," said Mort. "There's a lesion in your right retina. It looks like a small area of atrophy. You're a pathologist, you know the sorts of things that can cause focal atrophy."

His words triggered an immediate rush. It was like an internal alert circuit had been activated. I felt like I had antennae, and they were out searching for signals.

Edwards looked at me. "I'm want to have Mike Murphy to take a look at your eye." I could feel my adrenalin flowing. "Mike Murphy," I thought, "he's a neurosurgeon who specializes in brain tumors. I've autopsied some of his patients."

I felt tension in the muscles of my forearms and hands, then realized I had strangle-holds on the arms of the chair. I told myself: "Relax," but that didn't work. I felt the flutter behind my sternum. My ventricles were pumping faster and vibrating. I could hear the air moving deeper in my chest with each breath.

"Be right back," said Mort stepping out into the hallway with Edwards.

Alone for a moment, thoughts raced past, but I couldn't hold onto them. It was like my brain was scanning files, rapidly opening one, for an instant displaying it, then before I could focus, closing the file and moving on to the next. I felt like the parts of my brain that controlled intellect were saying: "Stay calm!" but the parts that controlled viscera and emotion were not listening.

When Murphy arrived he examined the retinas and agreed there was a suspicious lesion in the right retina. "We're not going to know what's going on here until we get a brain CT scan," Murphy said. "I'll get one scheduled for tomorrow morning."

Murphy left and Mort began: "Richard, I've talked this over with Ed and Mike and we all agree that the lesion on your retina is worrisome. You know the list of possible causes, none of them are good. We are particularly concerned that you may have a brain tumor.

Since there are no other symptoms, if a tumor is there, it is probably very small. It's also possible that this is a solitary lesion of Multiple Sclerosis, but that is less likely."

As he spoke, I began to feel panic and an intense alertness. Scenarios and *what-ifs* raced through my mind. For an instant a thought would appear, then its implications, then derivatives of the implications; then they were gone and a new thought appeared. It was like my brain was stuck in fast forward while an internal synthesizer built mental pyramids of actions and consequences, but so fast and so complex, that I couldn't keep track. I had the feeling of being trapped in a chess game where each time I considered a strategy, before I could think it out, a second strategy appeared, displacing the first, then a third strategy would emerge and replace the second. As much as I tried, I couldn't stop the mental barrage. My internal synthesizer was out of control; my pause button didn't work.

"In the absence of any other symptoms, that lesion on your retina is a big puzzle to all of us," said Mort. "I don't have to tell you that the lesion means there are some dead neurons in that retina. Excluding a long list of genetic and systemic diseases, none of which you have, when a person your age develops a focus of retinal atrophy it usually reflects a lesion back in the brain. The only other reasonable possibility is a previous traumatic injury."

"Have you ever had a head injury or an eye injury?"

"No, I've been pretty healthy all my life."

"When you were a kid did you ever look directly at the sun, or have you ever used binoculars or a telescope to look at a solar eclipse? Those things can burn a retina and cause this kind of a lesion".

"No, I never did any of those things, but your question reminds me of something. I had an incredible visual experience in the Navy."

"I was at Bikini in 1956 and witnessed the testing of 17 hydrogen bombs. One of the bombs had a destructive force 300 times greater than the bomb dropped on Hiroshima. When it exploded I was sitting on an upper deck of the ship with my back to Ground Zero which was about 15 miles away. I was wearing safety goggles, had my face buried in my elbow and my elbow tucked between my folded knees. We had been told that when the bomb exploded we wouldn't see anything, but when it exploded I saw the bones in my arm, my radius and ulna."

"Wow! That's an amazing story," responded Mort. "It's possible that the flash from a hydrogen bomb could have injured your retina. The lesion has an appearance that is consistent with an old photo-thermal injury."

That an old injury might account for the lesion raised my hopes.

* * *

All that evening I fixated on my family and pondered what needed to get done if the CT scan found a tumor growing in my brain. Malignant brain tumors have a bleak prognosis. My wife Nancy and I didn't have any savings or home equity. We had three children, ages 10, 8 and 5. I didn't have life insurance. Only 3 years before, at age 38, after 14 years of college, medical school and residency training, I finally had a job with a salary. We were still repaying student loans. I felt desperate.

I wanted to tell Nancy about my afternoon in the eye clinic, but that had to wait. Next morning, while the CT scanner probed the inside of my skull, she would be taking a final exam in an engineering course. I didn't want to distract her with more stress.

Sleep never came that night. As I laid in the dark, *what-if* scenarios cascaded through my mind. Some triggered fear and I tried to suppress them, but they kept returning. I thought about Nancy and our children, Alison, Brendan and Matthew. Tears began to well at the thought we might never again canoe an Ozark river, lay together on one of its gravel bars searching the night sky for Orion and Pleiades, and awake in the morning fog to the sounds of a running river and wild turkeys fussing in the nearby woods. I winced at the thought of never again hiking a trail in the Tetons carrying one of our children on my back.

*　*　*

Next morning in the softly-lit radiology suite, I lay immobilized, bound by Velcro straps to a moving platform, feeling tense and vulnerable as motors humming in the background slowly inserted me into the tubular core of the CT scanner. As my body entered the narrow passage, a wave of light headedness eclipsed my apprehension. I felt weightless and floating in and out of a twilight zone. Confused, I groped for orientation. Suddenly, psychedelic images began racing through my mind. I saw myself standing in the shadows inside a compartment in a submarine watching the crew prepare to fire torpedoes. Then I realized it was me—not a torpedo—strapped to the carriage that slowly moved along the conveyor and disappeared inside of the firing chamber. I screamed in horror knowing that in a moment I would be blasted out of existence. The crew didn't hear my screams. They sealed the chamber door and I was gone.

Then the scene changed and I saw myself standing inside of a cancer cell in my brain frantically battling with sinuous, octopus-like giant chromosomes that lashed at me and wrapped around my chest and legs. I grabbed the writhing coils of DNA and tried to peal them free. I battered at the chromosomes with my head and sank my teeth into them, but they kept replicating like the brooms in *The Sorcerer's Apprentice*. I tore at the strands of DNA wrapped around my neck strangling me, as my eyes, now extruded from their sockets and dangling on long stalks, futilely watched my demise.

Then the scene changed and I saw myself lying on a steel tray in a morgue. An attendant tied a tag to my right big toe. The tag had my name on it. Then he began to slide the tray into one of the shelves of the cooler. I tried to tell him I wasn't dead, but my lips wouldn't move. He pulled the sheet over my face, closed the door and at once, all was dark and cold.

"Remember, doctor: Don't move during the procedure!", yelled the radiology technician from across the room, breaking my delirium. "We won't get good images if you move."

As the scanner moved through each step of its programmed routine, soft mechanical and electronic sounds of its movements came from all around me. Inside my head a tense conversation with myself frantically repeated.

"I need to lay out everything that needs to get done if it's a brain tumor."

"It can't be a brain tumor, I didn't have any symptoms."

"But small brain tumors can be silent."

"In a few hours, I'll know what it is."

"Maybe it's from Bikini."

"It can't be. None of the Bikini vets developed brain tumors."

"Maybe this is the first."

"If it's a tumor, how much time will I have?"

Then the cycle repeated: "I need to lay out everything............"

Suddenly, the sounds stopped, the lights came back on, and the technologist returned.

"All finished, doctor. I'll have you out of there in a minute."

* * *

I walked to my lab fixated on the scan, desperate to know what it showed. In my mind I could see panels of CT films mounted on the wall of a dark room. A group of physicians stared at the images, sometimes pointing at the shadows on the films, shadows of the inside of my skull, shadows that held the answer. Soon there would be a decision and a radiologist would dictate the report. Soon I would hear from Mort. I wanted the morning to be over.

I entered my office and found a list of phone calls to return. On my desk was a stack of correspondence needing signatures. Two students awaited my arrival, anxious to discuss the results of some experiments. I wanted to immerse myself in lab matters, thinking it would hasten the passage of time, but thoughts of the scan kept intruding. As I listened to the students, I found myself pondering their fate, and that of the entire lab team, if the scan showed a tumor. After about 40 minutes I made some suggestions to the students and our meeting ended. As they left I wondered if my preoccupation had shown.

I returned a few phone calls and started signing the correspondence. Then the phone rang. I felt the adrenaline rush. My heart pounded and I reflexly tensed. I took a deep breath and picked up the receiver. "Dr. Lynch, could you come down the hall and take a look in the microscope at these new cells?"

I let the deep breath escape. It was Ruth, the chief research assistant in the lab.

"I'll be right there," I said. I walked to the lab, sat at the scope and began studying the flask of cells Ruth had placed on the microscope.

"How do they look to you?", she asked.

The flask contained a unique line of cancer cells that I had obtained from a colleague in Germany who had created them. My research team was excited because the cells would allow us to perform critical experiments that previously were not possible. The cells he let us have were to revolutionize biomedical research. Ten years later he received a Nobel Prize for his work.

"Ruth, this is fantastic!" I said. "They look great. I can see some of them dividing".

When cells are shipped long distances many of them die, and those that survive act like they've been shocked and cease dividing. Leaving the constant environment of a warm incubator in Freiberg, Germany, bouncing about in mail trucks and jetliner cargo bins, sitting in cold airport freight rooms waiting for their next flight, or for customs inspectors to approve entry, all take a toll on the viability of cultured cells. In our lab Ruth had the reputation of having "magic hands". It was a rare cell line that she could not get to grow.

My excitement at her success with the new cell line temporarily suppressed all thoughts of CT scans and brain tumors.

Several members of the lab heard the excited conversation and joined us. We spent about an hour discussing how to proceed with the cells, and outlining the first generation of experiments As we finished up and I started back to my office, thoughts of the CT scan returned, and the irony struck me—joy that cancer cells were dividing in a plastic flask; fear that others might be dividing in my brain.

Stepping out of the lab I reflexly flinched when I saw Mort at the end of the hallway, heading my way. My apprehension and fear were instant. His steps quickened when he saw me. Then I saw the telling smile. I knew he had good news.

He slapped my shoulder, grabbed my hand and excitedly said: "Your scan was negative." I felt I had just been given back my life. I couldn't wait to go home.

When I arrived home and told Nancy about the events of the last two days, she was thrilled about the outcome but disappointed that I had not told her before. I said, "I didn't want to distract you from studying for your final exam." She said, "You're not going to believe this, but I walked into that exam room and everything was a blank. I've never done that before."

"I bet you aced it," I said. Nancy had a straight A record in the course. A week later she got her grade in the mail and then phoned me in the lab. "You must have been sending out vibes," she said. "How's that," I said. "I blew the final."

CHAPTER 14

Oskar

I glanced at my watch. It read 11:15 p.m. His flight was due to land in fifteen minutes. It had been more than twenty-four hours since he left Moscow's Sheremetyevo Airport headed for New York's JFK. I'd been waiting at Gate 17 for two hours. I had come early just to be safe. I couldn't imagine what would happen if I missed him.

For an airport in the middle of the desert this late on a weekday night, the place was humming. It was as crowded as a terminal at Chicago's O'Hare the day before a holiday weekend. But this was not an O'Hare crowd—no business men and women in suits, cramped into rows of plastic bucket seats staring like zombies at laptops; or college students toting backpacks, their baseball caps turned backwards; or young couples, one pushing a child in a fold-up stroller, the other carrying a sleeping infant. This was a different crowd—tanned, well-built, silver-haired guys in wide-brimmed, pearly white Stetsons wearing designer jeans and flashy-stitched cowboy boots unlikely to ever touch the inside of a stirrup; groups of cigarette-smoking, blue-tinted, silver-haired grandmas in sequin-spattered tee shirts, tell-tales of an ocean cruise or a trip to Disneyland; and departing conventioneers busily feeding coins into slot machines and pulling handles, hoping for some last minute luck before heading home to Fargo, Grand Rapids, and Harrisburg.

Announcements blaring from loudspeakers added to the background ruckus of conversations and laughter, and from time to time a shriek went up when a slot machine flashed colored lights, sounded bells and whistles, and with the staccato beat of a woodpecker drumming on a tree, spewed coins into a tin pan. At 11:30 p.m. the loudspeakers announced what I had been waiting to hear: "United flight 31 from New York has just landed. Arriving passengers can be met at Gate 17."

The events that took me to Gate 17 at the Las Vegas International Airport had begun four years earlier, in June of 1984 in Moscow. A colleague of mine from Hungary introduced me to Oskar at a vodka-saturated reception hosted by Soviet scientists to welcome lecturers who had been invited to Moscow from overseas. I had several conversations with Oskar that week. He told me about his research on proteins produced by the malignant cells in patients with multiple myeloma, a subject close to my own research interests. I learned that he had been raised in a secular Jewish family in Kiev in the Ukraine, had earned a doctorate in chemistry, and worked as a scientist at the Cardiovascular Institute in Moscow. Until we met, I knew nothing of Oskar's work because during the Cold War the Soviet government prohibited scientists from publishing papers in western journals. I soon realized that in spite of working in an isolated, confining environment with limited resources, Oskar had made some interesting findings.

I met Oskar again at a symposium in Hungary in the summer of 1987. He asked me if I would carry a vial of protein and a letter back to the United States and get them to Professor Alan Solomon, a friend of mine who directed the Cancer Center at the University of Tennessee in Knoxville. Oskar said that if he mailed the vial and the letter within the Soviet Union he ran the risk of being accused of espionage. He had never met or communicated with Professor Solomon, but he knew that Alan was a world authority on the proteins made by myeloma cells. I agreed to take the materials. When I sent the package to Alan I told him about Oskar, saying that Oscar was a first-rate scientist but, as with other Jewish scientists in the Soviet Union, the Soviet government refused to allow him to travel beyond the Iron Curtain.

Two days before I stood waiting for Oskar at Gate 17, I had received a phone call from Washington in my office in Iowa City as I was preparing to come to Las Vegas for the congress. Unbeknownst to me, Alan Solomon was a close friend of Howard Baker, then Chief of Staff in the Reagan White House. The caller explained that the White House had arranged for Oskar to come to the United States to work with Professor Solomon for six months. However, after all the arrangements had been made for Oskar to travel from Moscow to Knoxville, someone suggested that since Oskar had never been to a large scientific congress in the United States and Alan would be in Las Vegas, Oskar should go to Las Vegas, attend the congress, and then travel with Alan back to Tennessee. Last minute efforts to contact Oskar in Moscow and tell him of the change in plans were unsuccessful. The caller knew that I had met Oskar and knew that I was going to be at the congress in Las Vegas. Since I knew what Oskar looked like, the called said, would I go to the Las Vegas airport, meet Oskar, and take him to his hotel. The caller said that arrangements had been made to have Oskar met when he deplaned in New York and tell him of the change in plans. Oskar had departed Moscow believing he was headed for Knoxville, Tennessee.

As passengers began exiting through Gate 17 I studied each face without finding Oskar's. After the main bolus of passengers had cleared the gate and only stragglers and passengers in wheel chairs continued to exit, I began to worry. For a couple of moments the flow of passengers ceased and then crew members appeared, pulling their luggage behind them on wheelies. "He must have missed the connection in New York," I thought. And then I saw him, walking behind two flight attendants, a weathered leather school bag hanging on a strap from one of his shoulders. As he moved down the jet way he seemed to slink behind the two crew members, as if they were his shield. As he exited the gate, his eyes fixed and intense, he scanned the surroundings like a deer at the forest's edge searching an open field before venturing forward. Then he saw me and for the first time ever, I saw Oskar smile. He ran to me and threw his arms around me.

"You can't believe how happy I am to see you," he said. "When I got off the plane in New York two women were there holding signs with my name on them. I went up to them and they told me that plans had changed and I had to go to Las Vegas, instead of Tennessee. I knew something was wrong. One of the women spoke Russian. I was terrified. She told me that many scientists were in Las Vegas and one of them—she didn't know who—would meet me at the airport. I knew that Las Vegas had nothing to do with science, so I was sure these women were part of a KGB trap. I didn't know what to do. They had changed my tickets and insisted that I go to Las Vegas. It seemed I had no choice."

Then Oskar told me he had a vial of live cells inside his leather bag. To keep the cells alive he had placed the thimble-sized vial into a Styrofoam cup filled with ice that he had continued to replenish during the trip. I told him that when we got to the hotel there would not be problem keeping the cells cold. He claimed his luggage and we headed for the taxi stand outside. Without getting out of the vehicle, the driver popped the trunk and I put Oskar's suitcase inside. It was a bit after midnight when we got into the back seat of the taxi and told the driver to take us to the Hilton. Our driver was a gorgeous blond woman, probably in her late twenties, who had a long braided ponytail. She wore a tight black tee shirt that emphasized her mammalian form, a bright red monogrammed baseball cap, and stylish dark sunglasses that made it impossible to see her eyes. When she pulled away from the curb a row of tiny, multi-colored lights that rimmed the brim of her cap began flashing in an amazing array of patterns.

In minutes our cab entered the neon-lit festive world of casinos, hotels, resorts, and avenues lined with crowded sidewalks. Our driver chatted non-stop pointing out motels with drive-in marriage chapels, the best places to eat, and the casinos with the friendliest slot machines. Oskar seemed overwhelmed by the scene outside, but remained silent. I'd never been to Las Vegas before and was experiencing a bit of culture shock myself. As our cab zipped along the Las Vegas Strip, beams of colored light flashed across Egyptian Pyramids, medieval castles, the walls of the Grand Canyon, and miniatures of the Eiffel Tower, the Statue of Liberty, and the Tower of London. Columns of water danced above the fountains of Rome, and Venetian sailors poled gondolas along canals. The scene couldn't have differed more from the drab, gray, barren streets of Moscow at one in the morning. I wondered what was going on inside of Oskar's head.

When we reached the lobby of the Hilton the place was mobbed. About 60 people stood in five lines waiting to register at the hotel. Slot machines lined the room; some people were feeding coins into three machines, moving from one to another depositing coins and pulling handles Along one wall a bride, groom, and bridal party, all in formal attire and loosened by champagne, frolicked while feeding coins and pulling handles. Oskar and I got in line at the front desk. After about 20 minutes Oskar began to fret about his vial of live cells. It was past 1:00 a.m. and I knew that Alan would be sleeping, but I decided to phone him to see if we could get a bucket of ice and leave the vial in his room. Alan told me to wait in the lobby and he would call the hotel manager to find a safe place for the cells. After about fifteen minutes a hotel staff member walked through the lobby calling out, "Professor Rokhlin!" I waved and the man came up to Oskar and me and said, "You don't need to wait in line to register. We will take care of that for you. Please follow me, I'll take you to your room." When we arrived at Oskar's room two men were easing a large refrigerator\freezer strapped to a dolly through the doorway. The scene epitomized Las Vegas excess. Oskar placed the thimble-sized vial into the spacious refrigerator. I told him I would be back at 8:00 a.m. to take him to breakfast.

Next morning I took Oskar to meet Alan and left them to breakfast together. I had a full day of conferences and presentations ahead of me. Oskar planned to attend some symposia and view the scientific exhibits. I told him I would meet him in our hotel lobby at 7:00 p.m. and we would go to dinner together. As I went about my schedule during the day, I worried about Oskar getting lost in the enormous convention center and wondered how he would react to some of the oddities he would encounter if he wandered away from the scientific sessions. At mid-afternoon the walls of the convention hall rumbled, chandeliers swayed overhead, and a deafening boom sounded. "It's a nuclear attack!" I heard someone in the room say. A scientist sitting next to me took a tiny radio out of his jacket pocket, turned it on, and held it to his ear. After a few moments he turned to me and said that there had been a gigantic explosion at a munitions factory in Henderson, Nevada, which is close to Las Vegas. I was sure that, being jet-lagged and in strange new surroundings, Oskar would have been bewildered and stressed when he heard the explosion. The blast triggered memories in me of conversations in Moscow where Oskar told me that Russians were worried about nuclear attacks from the United States, and I told him that Americans were worried about Russian nuclear-armed missiles arriving in North America.

When I arrived in the lobby that evening I was relieved to find that all my concerns about Oskar had been for naught. I found him feeding quarters into a slot machine with one hand, pulling the handle with the other, and watching the dials spin. He looked as acclimated to Las Vegas as the rows of senior citizens to his left and right.

At the end of the congress Oskar went with Alan to Tennessee. Oskar did well in Knoxville. After six months he returned to Moscow and when the Soviet Union collapsed he came to the United States with his family and became a U.S. citizen. I recruited him to the University of Iowa where he is a Professor in the Department of Pathology and continues his cancer research. In Iowa City Oskar became interested in his Jewish ancestry. He studied Hebrew and became a devout, observant member of his synagogue.

After I retired I often met Oskar for coffee when I was in the medical center. One afternoon I went to see him after my chemotherapy treatment in the cancer center. I wanted to get his recollection of some of the events during the five days we spent in Las Vegas. We spent about an hour together and as we finished up I asked him what he remembered about the taxi ride from the airport. He answered, "I remember that the driver hardly had any clothes on."

CHAPTER 15

Contrasts

Each Christmas Eve as I pick my way through boxes of entangled ornaments, many collected over the years from distant places, and more decorations than one tree can hold, I come across five that have special meaning. Made of wood from an olive tree, each ornament contains a nativity scene delicately carved into the wood by a Palestinian craftsman. As I search the tree for a place to hang them, my thoughts go back to Bethlehem.

In 1991 I accepted an invitation to present a lecture at the International Biochemistry Congress in Jerusalem. The invitation arrived at a very busy time and just as Rafael Nunez, a postdoctoral fellow in the lab had made an interesting discovery about a gene involved in allergic reactions. I felt his discovery merited presentation at one of the workshops held during the Congress. A pediatrician from Columbia, Rafael had come to the United States to get advanced research training.

"Rafael," I said, "how would you like to go to a meeting in Israel to present your work?" He looked at me in disbelief. "There are funds in one of the grants that will cover all your expenses," I continued. I could tell from his face he would have left for Israel within the hour.

"I've got a busy several weeks coming up, " I told him. "It would help me—and I think it would be a good experience for you—to make some of the arrangements," I said. We can travel and room together. I'll have the travel office take care of making the airline reservations. You can find a place for us to stay. I'll give you the information packet the congress organizers sent to me It has a list of accommodations in Jerusalem."

Two weeks later Rafael told me we were all set. He had a place for us in Jerusalem.

* * *

As our El Al flight approached Tel Aviv I asked Rafael if he knew how to get to the hotel. "I have a map," he said. "When we get to Jerusalem we will need to get a taxi. I found a real good deal at a pension. They wanted $200 a night at the Hilton and the King David Hotel. The pension costs $14 a night, and that includes breakfast."

I had visions of a Spartan shelter and wondered if I should have made the hotel arrangements and not left them to a trainee who lived on a tight budget.

"How close is the hostel to the convention center?" I asked.

"About a 20 minute ride on a city bus. Our pension is right across the street from the Yad Vashem Holocust Museum."

The pension consisted of several dormitory buildings surrounding a large central courtyard containing a scattering of benches, tables and a few palm trees. The manager, an outgoing Israeli, handed us sheets, pillows and towels and showed us to our room. The small, clean chamber contained two sets of bunk beds, one chair, a small closet and some nails on the wall for hanging garments.

After a snack at a local falafel shop and a walk through the neighborhood, we returned to the pension to find the courtyard teeming with orthodox Jewish families. The manager told us that, except for Rafael and me, all the pension guests were immigrants, just arrived from the Soviet Union. Several men were playing balalaikas and most of the adults were singing along in Russian.

As Rafael and I sat listening to the singing, long shadows created by the setting sun, and gentle, cool breezes moved across the courtyard. The music had a serious but folksy character. During one of the pieces a voice came from overhead. I looked up and saw a bearded man, a shawl around his shoulders, standing on the roof of a dormitory, booming his basso profundo out over the courtyard. It was like a scene from an opera. I was glad that Rafael had not booked us at the Hilton or the King David.

We returned to our room and before turning in for the night we spent some time going over Rafael's workshop presentation scheduled for the following day. I elected to take the upper bunk and Rafael the lower. Twenty four hours of airplanes and airports made it easy to fall asleep.

In the middle of the night I awoke to loud talking and commotion as two Russian men arrived to take the other two bunk beds. When the lights were turned off and quiet returned, I again fell asleep. Later, I awoke to what seemed angry shouting in Russian, doors slamming, luggage banging and the noisy departure of our two roommates. I looked at my watch and it was 3:00 a.m.

At breakfast next morning I mentioned to the manager about the late arrival of two men and wondered about all the commotion and their noisy departure in the middle of the night. I asked him if he knew what had happened. He looked at me and said: "One of you guys is a terrible snorer."

Rafael was interested in visiting Bethlehem which is located in the West Bank about six miles from Jerusalem. I asked an Israeli colleague about making a visit to Bethlehem. He told me that at the present time getting there was a bit complicated and advised against making the trip because of safety concerns due to unrest on the West Bank. When he saw we still wanted to go, he explained the procedure and gave us directions.

Like many of the Israelis I met, he deplored the violence and the restrictions and conditions imposed on Palestinians, and expressed the opinion that a minority of Arab and Israeli extremists were responsible for the turmoil.

After obtaining security clearance Rafael and I boarded a dusty, old school bus headed in the direction of Bethlehem. Steel grates, most of them deformed from past encounters with thrown rocks covered every window of the bus. Some windows contained shattered cracks. The bus was crowded with Israeli soldiers. Rafael and I were the only non-military passengers. The Israeli soldiers carried rifles, Uzis and other pieces of equipment.

Officially, bus service from Jerusalem to Bethlehem did not exist. When the bus reached the outskirts of Bethlehem it stopped and let us off. For security reasons a wall surrounded Bethlehem. The bus driver pointed to a gate in the wall and told us to walk there and speak with the soldier guarding the entrance. Immediately inside the security gate stood the tomb of the biblical matriarch Rachel, wife of Jacob and mother of Joseph and Benjamin. The third holiest site in Judaism, until the Six Day War in 1968 Jews had been forbidden to visit Rachel's Tomb.

After inspecting our passports and permits to visit, the guard gave us directions to Manger Square and the Church of the Nativity. It was about a 30 minute walk along a narrow residential street. Children waved and some adults nodded and smiled as we made our way through their neighborhood. About half way along a man who had been standing in a doorway watching us approach, came into the street and in perfect English welcomed us and asked if we needed any help. When he learned I was American he seemed very happy, shook my hand and invited us to come into his home and meet his family.

Rafael and I entered the small, comfortable dwelling where his wife insisted that we stay for tea. He proudly showed family pictures and spoke of some relatives who lived in Detroit and his hope to someday visit the United States. He advised us about shops that had good prices and made recommendations about safety. As we left he introduced us to friendly neighbors who had gathered outside of his home, curious about his foreign guests. The warmth and welcome of everyone we met as we walked through the neighborhood relieved the anxiety created by Uzis and steel grates on shattered bus windows.

When we reached Manger Square we learned that the Church of the Nativity sat over a grotto thought to be the site of Jesus' birth. As I purchased admission tickets I happened to look up and see that atop of Bethlehem's City Hall stood six Israeli soldiers armed with Uzis and perusing the scene below.

Inside the church we learned that battles over turf had not been left at the church door. Different parts of the church interior were under strict jurisdiction of Greek Orthodox, Armenian Rite and Roman Catholic factions of Christianity. Contentious struggles over turf by various factions of Catholicism date from before the time of the First Crusades and involve not only the site of Christ's birth, but also the site of his death.

As I flew back to the United States I thought about the contrasts between people and institutions.

CHAPTER 16

Freedom Lessons

FOR 96 MILES TWO CONCRETE WALLS encircled West Berlin, the space between them a *No Man's Land*. Berliners called that space *the death strip*—rows of barbed wire, concrete barriers, machine gun towers, impediments that triggered sirens when touched, and a fenced corridor guarded by attack dogs. Powerful flood lamps sat above on wooden poles; broken bottles and trash littered the ground below.

As our bus moved through *No Man's Land*, from behind me I heard Frau Muller, the conference secretariat telling someone: "When I came through here last month, a bouquet of flowers lie on the ground right over there."

On board sat 20 scientists from around the world, invited to West Berlin to produce in one week a book addressing the major unanswered questions in leukemia research. The German foundation that organized and sponsored the meeting provided every conceivable resource needed to make such an ambitious goal possible.

Except for a free afternoon in the middle of the week, our daily format demanded total commitment to the task—early morning starts; working through meals; adjourning after dark; assignments due the following morning. Because of the pressing agenda, invitees had been instructed to come to Berlin alone. All complied except the scientist from Poland. She arrived accompanied by a Polish secret service agent. During the entire week, they appeared inseparable.

At the request of our group, the foundation had made arrangements to visit the Pergamon Museum in East Berlin during our free afternoon. The Pergamon houses an extraordinary collection of artistic treasures from Greek and Roman antiquity, Babylonian culture, and the Islamic world. The geography and politics of 1983 Germany complicated traveling the few miles between our meeting site and the Pergamon.

At the East Berlin entry point an Uzi-armed border guard entered the bus, collected our passports, then left. As we waited, through the bus windows we watched the astonishing scene taking place outside. Passengers from vehicles returning to West Berlin stood in the roadway while border guards rolled what looked like old-fashioned lawn mowers under their vehicles. Instead of cutting blades, the equipment held mirrors that allowed the guards to view the undercarriage of the vehicle. They were looking for people attempting to escape from East Germany.

Our passports returned, two East German security agents boarded the bus and remained with us for the afternoon. Without a word they walked behind as we toured the museum. After leaving the Pergamon our bus stopped at a small café in a park, a state coffee shop exclusively serving foreigners and only accepting western currency. Its location prevented contact between visitors and East German citizens.

Back at the border crossing, the bus emptied and we joined a line entering one end of a small building. Inside, an Uzi-armed border guard scrutinized the face before him and the face in the passport photo, then slowly thumbed through the pages. Without a word or change in robotic expression, he handed the passport back and motioned with his head to pass. Guards with German Shepherds searched inside the bus while others used their mirrors on wheels to check for humans who might be clinging to the underside of the bus.

Back in our seats, the East German Security agents gone, our bus slowly moved through *No Man's Land* along a strikingly zigzagging road, a road designed to impede any vehicles that might attempt escape by crashing through the border check point.

A colleague sitting cross the aisle broke the silence. A distinguished scientist originally from Budapest and now working in Stockholm, years before he had jumped from a train filled with other Jews headed for Auschwitz.

"I hope everyone noticed," he commented "they only use the mirrors to check vehicles leaving the country. People aren't trying to sneak into East Germany."

CHAPTER 17

A Priceless Payment

FOUR YEARS INTO OUR RETIREMENT my wife and I flew to Costa Rica to spend eighteen days searching for and photographing some of the more than 800 species of birds that reside there. On a February afternoon we left the Iowa winter behind and flew to San Jose. After a week on our own we joined twelve other birders in an Elderhostel group and spent the next 10 days visiting some of Costa Rica's birding hotspots.

Our final stop before returning home was San Gerardo de Dota in the Talamanca Mountains about 40 miles south of San Jose. We came here hoping to see and photograph the Resplendent Quetzal, a bird sacred to the ancient Maya and Aztecs and today considered the most beautiful bird in the Western Hemisphere.

The tropical cloud forest of the Savegre River Valley around San Gerardo de Dota is an ecological treasure. The forest of massive oaks and other native trees is home to more than 170 species of birds, including many endemics. Birders come to the Savegre River Valley from all over the world hoping to see the Resplendent Quetzal, a spectacular bird whose numbers continue to decline because of widespread deforestation throughout its range in Central and South America. About 1000 acres of the forest along the Savegre River around San Gerardo de Dota is a protected sanctuary containing

80% of virgin growth, the rest being native species planted in a reforestation program. The sanctuary contains five different ecosystems and was developed by the Chacon family, the first settlers in the valley and the owners of the hotel where we stayed. Scientists from around the world use the sanctuary as a living research laboratory dedicated to preserving the precious diversity of plant and animal life in tropical cloud forests. San Gerardo de Dota is one of the few places in Costa Rica where birders have a reasonable chance of seeing the Resplendent Quetzal.

The final four miles of our trip to San Gerardo de Dota had its share of white-knuckle moments. After exiting the Pan American Highway at an altitude of 10,000 feet, our driver navigated the minibus down a 3,000-foot descent on a steep, narrow dirt road full of switchbacks and unguarded cliffs. When you peer out the side window of your minibus and can't see the road's edge, you know you're pretty close. As we made our way down the winding road, I wondered what would happen if we met a vehicle coming from the opposite direction. Luckily, I never found out.

Thanks to Edwin Ramirez, our sharp-eyed guide, our stop at San Gerardo de Dota was rewarded on the first morning with close-up views of five Quetzals, two of them males in spectacular breeding plumage. The bright morning light and clear mountain air made ideal conditions for photographing quetzals as they fed in a wild avocado grove, flashing their brilliant red, green, and blue colors as they flew from tree to tree.

Following a successful morning of photographing Resplendent Quetzals we spent the rest of the day hiking up and down steep trails and stretching our necks backwards to search the forest canopy for other exotic birds. At sunset we returned to the hotel, excited about the splendid birds we had photographed and ready for a soft chair and something cool to sip. Relieved to be out of heavy hiking boots and into cool sandals, I stood at the tiny crowded bar of our hotel just before dinner, trying to get the bartender's attention and hoping that his cooler contained a bottle of chardonnay. The Savegre Hotel de Montana was fully booked and its lounge buzzed with conversations as birders talked about Collared Trogons, Ochraceous Wrens, Torrent Tyranulets, Emerald Toucanets, and other exotic birds seen during the day. Looking to my right, hoping to catch the bartender's eye when he finished pouring a pina colada, I noticed a handsome, snowy-haired woman, probably in her mid-seventies, sitting on a bar stool, engaged in serious conversation with a middle-aged gentleman. She caught my attention because she was pointing at two lesions on her exposed right shin. The surface of her shin contained two oozing, hemorrhagic abrasions, the largest one the size of a credit card, the smaller one about half that size. The skin from the large rectangular abrasion had been torn away and hung as a flap attached to the surrounding skin only along one edge. As a physician I recognized the serious nature of her injury. At any age, but especially at hers, it required immediate attention.

 The bartender asked for my order, then extended my day of good fortune by reaching for a bottle of Chilean chardonnay and pouring two glasses. I carried them to the table where my wife Nancy sat. I told her about the woman's wounds and asked about the supply of antibiotics in our first aid kit. Nancy said we had some penicillin and azithromycin. When the conversing gentleman left the woman to join friends at a table, I approached her, told her I was a physician, and inquired about her wounds. She told me she was in Costa Rica with a birding group and that two hours ago, in spite of walking with the help of a cane, she had taken a bad fall on a steep trail. I asked what she had done to treat the wounds and learned she had cleaned them and applied a topical antibiotic ointment. Those were excellent first steps, but I was concerned about the development of a potentially life-threatening complication. If the wound was contaminated—an almost certainty given the conditions of the rain forest floor—microbes could enter her blood stream and spread throughout her body. Blood stream infections, especially in the elderly, can prove fatal. When I learned that she had an implanted cardiac pacemaker and an artificial knee, that made it all the more urgent she begin antibiotic treatment. I told her I had some antibiotics and recommended that she begin taking them right away to prevent a systemic infection. When bacteria gain access to the blood stream they have a predilection to lodge on prosthetic devices such as pacemakers and artificial joints. Eliminating bacteria before they start growing on an implanted device is critical. Once infection occurs—without surgical intervention to remove the infected hardware—the patient has a poor chance of surviving. I asked if she had ever taken penicillin, and she told me she was allergic to it. I was glad that we also had some azithromycin in our first aid kit. Nancy returned to our room and retrieved the antibiotics. I gave the woman enough azithromycin for a complete course of treatment.

The next morning I felt relieved when I saw her sitting at a table eating breakfast and looking well. I gave her some sterile adhesive bandages and told her to change them daily, to continue taking the azithromycin and applying the topical antibiotic, and to contact her physician as soon as she returned to the United States. She said she felt that I had saved her life, and she wanted to pay me. I told her that the pleasure that came from being able to help her, and seeing her looking so well this morning, were more than enough payment. Besides, I told her, I was only licensed to practice medicine in Iowa, not in Costa Rica. As I started to take her leave and head for the breakfast line, she arose from her chair and gestured discreetly that she wanted to speak with me in private. Taking me by the arm, she slowly walked me away from her table. Out of the earshot of others, she leaned towards me and whispered, "If you won't allow me to give you money, let me pay you with a bird." Then she added, "But you have to promise that you won't tell anyone else about it until after our group leaves."

Continuing to whisper, she said, "You must be a photographer. I saw you outside this morning trying to photograph a Long-tailed Silky Flycatcher." Shooting a quick glance at the table where the rest of her group sat eating breakfast, she continued, "Our group does a lot of birding trips together and on each trip we have a photo contest. The pictures are judged after we get back home. I took a great shot yesterday, but I don't want anyone else in my group to know about it because some of them will be over there taking the same picture." I guessed she had seen an unusual bird and was about to tell me where she saw it. I couldn't imagine why she seemed so confident that I would find the same bird. She continued to whisper, "Go over to cabin 123, stand on the porch with your back to the window, and look up." She stepped back, then touched my hand and said, "Thanks, again." Then she turned and walked back to her table.

After breakfast I hurried to cabin 123 and followed her instructions. Attached to the back of the light fixture mounted on the ceiling of the porch—inconspicuous to any but the most surveillant passerby—was a tiny nest. I concluded that my grateful patient must have seen an unusual bird at the nest. I decided to wait, hoping a bird would appear. As I stared at the nest I noticed slight movements of what I had assumed were the ends of strands of nesting material that barely protruded from the top of the nest. As I stood motionless and watched silently, a third piece of identical material appeared next to the other two. Lifting binoculars to my eyes I discovered that the thin, slightly curved straw-like structures extending from the top of the nest were tiny beaks. Excited, I shot several digital photos and left to find Nancy and show her the photos.

By next morning my benefactor and her group had departed. No longer bound by a vow of silence, I told two persons in our group about the nest and returned with them to cabin 123 after breakfast. As we stood quietly, taking photos and watching beaks appear and disappear, a gorgeous Green Violet-ear hummingbird arrived, alighted on the nest's edge, and began feeding the chicks. If the hummingbird noticed us, it did not appear to be concerned. We watched and shot photos of tiny, open beaks competing for the long tongue of their parent.

My thoughts returned to the snowy-haired woman who had dodged a life-threatening situation because I wanted a glass of chardonnay and Nancy had packed a second antibiotic. Being rewarded with close-up views of a Green Violet-ear hummingbird feeding its chicks has to be the most priceless payment I've received during 35 years in medicine.

Richard and his younger brother, Bill, at Macy's to see Santa and have their picture taken.

A family photograph from 1954, most likely sent to Richard while he was in the Navy. In the back, L to R is Jim Jr., Uncle Charlie, Aunt Anna, Uncle Joe, Mother (Helen Lynch), & sister Muriel Lynch. In front, sister Helen, brother Brian, and Father, James Lynch. The photograph was taken by Rich's brother, Bill.

Rich and friends.

Rich as a teenager.

The Camp Glen Hardie traveling van.

Richard as a young sailor soon after basic training.

Fishing was one of the favorite ways to pass time in Alaska.

Aboard ship in northern waters.

Recreation on the beaches at the time of Bikini bomb testing.

A mushroom cloud after one of the tests at Bikini.

Richard as a young scientist and faculty member in Pathology at the Washington University College of Medicine.

Richard and friend, trying on the headgear while in Jerusalem.

The Lynch siblings as adults: Back, L to R, Jim, Richard, Bill. Front, Brian, Muriel, and Helen.

Hummingbird nest, photographed by Richard after its location was disclosed by the grateful injured birder.

The University of Iowa official photograph of Dr. Richard G. Lynch, MD, Chair of Pathology from 1981 to 2000.

The Lynch Family: L to R Joan & Brendan, Matt & Daniale, Joey, Nancy, Alison, Richard. In front, Luis and Veronica. Photograph taken on June 21, 2009.

LOOKING BACK

Preface

As I approached retirement one of the things I looked forward to was having time to put on paper for my children and grandchildren some information about a part of their familial past. It was my hope that, just as I had always wanted to know more about my parents and grandparents, my children and their children might enjoy knowing more about some of their ancestors, and about my life and the many wonderful persons and experiences that influenced and enriched it.

I appreciate that with time a person's memory can prove to be selective and unreliable, and that it is easy for recollections to be colored by the way one wished things had been, rather than the way they were. Memoir writing runs the risk of transcending to fiction; I will try my best to be accurate and to avoid distortions.

Chapter One

My mother held a strong opinion about hospitals: they were where you went to die.

So when the first five of her children were born, they were delivered by my maternal grandmother, an old hand at home deliveries: all 15 of her children were born at home.

When I arrived in my parent's bedroom, it was April, 1934, the country was in the midst of the Great Depression, and President Franklin D. Roosevelt was early in his first term. My parents named me after my Uncle Richard, a quiet man with wanderlust, who as a teenager left home unannounced and spent two years incommunicado traveling with a circus. A widow with 14 other children, one severely mentally retarded, and all cramped into a 4 bedroom cold water flat without central heating, I doubt that Grandma spent all of those two years fretting about my Uncle Richie.

In 1944, at age 43, a complicated sixth pregnancy forced my mother to enter a hospital for the birth of my sister Mary. Born with severe hydrocephalus, she died several days later. For months afterwards, I often found my mother, her head slumped on a shoulder, sitting motionless in a chair by a window, drapes drawn and lamps unlit. In spite of the darkness, I could see the tears and reddened eyes. If I said something, she barely responded. Her mind was somewhere else. My father had told us that she would be sad, but seeing her that way made me sad, and frightened. Depression -a meaningless word to a ten year old- had ravaged her spirit.

About a year later another complicated pregnancy required hospitalization for the birth of my brother Brian, born with Down's Syndrome. Her physician painted a very bleak picture for Brian's further development and asked my parents if they wanted to make arrangements for Brian to be institutionalized. My mother, furious at the suggestion, refused to ever see that doctor again.

Devout Roman Catholics, never questioning what they heard from the pulpit, my parents believed that the sentinel events in life had divine purpose—behavior being punished; behavior being rewarded; one's faith in God being tested.

After Brian was born, fragments of conversations overheard made me realize that as my father anguished, he struggled with guilt, searching his past for transgressions that might explain why the Almighty had allowed Brian to be born with Down's Syndrome. I once overheard him say that after Brian's birth my grandmother, concerned about more pregnancies, sternly told him: "You stay away from that girl", a comment that likely did little to assuage his feelings of guilt, and a somewhat ironic command considering her own reproductive record.

A good argument could be made that the only reason my grandmother stopped at fifteen, was because her husband died during her last pregnancy. In those years childbirth was accompanied by significant maternal and infant mortality: it was an oddity that it was my grandfather who did not survive the pregnancy.

Until she died in 1962, my mother focused all of her energy and effort on nurturing Brian. As an infant flaccid, quiet, passive and slow to develop, when Brian did reach a milestone such as rolling over or sitting up, my parents saw it as a sign that up in the heavens their prayers and novenas were being heard, the votive candles they lit were being seen.

At age six, Brian began to attend a private school for developmentally handicapped children. The following year I left for four years in the Navy and, except for a few short periods, never again did I have the daily contact with him that most of my family enjoyed.

Brain made remarkable progress and by his teens had learned the rudiments of chess from his brother Bill. As his communication and social skills developed, it became evident that Brian possessed an extraordinary memory, especially for events—particularly embarrassing ones—that involved my father. Quite regularly a phrase in a nearby conversation would trigger Brian's memory and he would regale all present with the details of some family matter never intended for public discussion. If you wanted to know anything about anyone in the family, Brian was the guy to see.

Television was a boon to Brian's development. He loved to watch children's programs, comedy and sporting events, especially horse races and major league baseball games. When he learned to print, he wrote a daily calendar that included lists of upcoming television programs and kept a diary. He possessed a remarkably detailed knowledge of professional sporting events, especially horse races. Every evening he walked with my father to Maxie's newsstand to buy a copy of the New York Daily News, where listed within were the day's racing results and the race entries for the next day. Brian spent the rest of the evening at the kitchen table comparing the day's results to his predictions, and selecting his horses for the next day's races.

Occasionally, he had a big day of winners. When this happened, the entire neighborhood would know of it as Brian proudly spread the news while running errands for our mother. Everyone in the neighborhood knew Brian, and in spite of maternal admonitions to the contrary, he spoke with everyone he met. His attention to horse races became known to some of the older men in the neighborhood who regularly played the ponies. Some of them believed that the Almighty endowed mentally retarded children with special powers to compensate for their inherent limitations. Hoping that Brian might be so blessed, they frequently phoned our house to inquire about Brian's picks for the next day before placing their bets with a local bookie.

My mother would answer the phone and be asked whom Brian liked in the sixth race at Jamaica or the third race at Hialeah the next day. My mother held a puritanical view of gambling—the weekly Bingo games at the local parish hall she regularly attended excepted—these phone calls triggered her fears about the police arriving at her front door some day, investigating a gambling operation.

Brian died in 1991, at the age of 45. He belonged to that first generation of individuals with Down's Syndrome who, because of advances in medical care, attained such longevity. He was our family treasure.

Chapter Two

Born Helen Rita Henderson in 1901, my mother was the oldest of fifteen children. Six months after her father died in 1924, her mother gave birth to her last child and named her Muriel. Seven months later my mother gave birth to her first child, and named her Muriel. I never learned why my parents decided to also name my oldest sister Muriel. The two Muriels grew up together, went to the same school, lived within a few minute's walk of each other, but their relationship was always strained. From what I learned later on, having two little Muriels in the family, one an aunt, and the other a niece, created identity problems for each of them, and was a recipe for competitiveness and friction.

Finishing grade school, my mother worked as a telephone operator in a building that still stands in lower Manhattan, just blocks from where the World Trade Center was built decades later. Each day she walked the Brooklyn Bridge to save the price of the trolley fare. As her sisters completed grade school, they also went to work at the New York Telephone Company. Eventually four Henderson girls made the daily round trip walk across the Brooklyn Bridge.

I know little about my mother's ancestors except that her mother and father were born in Brooklyn; both grandfathers had come here from Ireland, and both grandmothers were first generation children of Irish immigrants. Her paternal grandfather was a detective on the New York City Police force who died at age 35 after being shot while responding to a burglary.

My father was born on Warren Street in 1897, a baseball's throw from where my mother lived, and four blocks from where I was born. He was the second of eight children. Both of his parents had been born in Brooklyn. His father worked as a lineman for a telegraph company. His paternal grandfather and grandmother were Irish immigrants. I never learned anything about the family of my father's mother.

When my father was twelve years old, his infant sister was fatally burned in a tragic accident involving the kerosene stove used to heat their flat. Most houses in their neighborhood lacked central heating. My grandmother never recovered from her devastating loss, and died two years later.

When my father was 19, his father died. Of the seven surviving children, four were old enough to live independently, but three were still considered too young to live on their own. My father and his brothers Ed, who was 22, and Bill, who was 14, moved into a flat four blocks away. His brother Frank, who was 17, joined the Army. During combat in World War I, he was one of thousands of American soldiers poisoned with nitrogen mustard gas, a weapon used by the German Army during brutal trench warfare in France. Frank returned home seriously ill, never recovered from the effects of the poison gas, and died from pulmonary failure a few years later.

My father's brothers Joe, who was 12, and George, who was 10, were sent to St. Vincent's Home for Orphaned Boys in downtown Brooklyn. As a teenager I remember hearing my uncles recall some of the sadistic methods—such as beatings with a rubber hose in the shower room—that were used by some of the staff to discipline boys at St. Vincent's Home. It sounded like a frightful, abusive place out of a 19th century novel, where order was maintained by fear and intimidation. My Aunt Lillie, who was 13, was sent to a Dominican convent in New Jersey. She never left the convent and spent the rest of her life as a Dominican nun.

Leaving high school after one year, my father went to work in Manhattan as "an office boy", where he performed a variety of chores and ran errands. He later recalled that finding employment was difficult because of his limited schooling, his lack of any marketable skills, and the occasional posted vacancies for unskilled workers that contained the caveat: "Irish need not apply".

He took evening classes in accounting at a business school in

Manhattan and this led to employment as a clerk in a firm that managed the family fortune inherited by descendants of one of the original partners of John D. Rockefeller. The office was located on Broadway near Wall Street, in a skyscraper just a couple of blocks from where the twin towers of the World Trade Center would be built many decades later.

When I was a child, my father was the first one up each morning and could be heard singing in the kitchen as he shaved. He made coffee, hustled to the local German bakery for muffins and biscuits, or to the local deli for hard rolls, and then was off to the subway, in a white shirt, tie, and three-piece suit. In the summer he wore a straw hat, and in the winter a fedora and an overcoat. After working a full day in Manhattan, he returned to Brooklyn to a part-time job as bookkeeper in a shoe store.

I never heard him complain about work, but I know from overheard conversations that there were times when income did not meet expenses, and not all of the household bills that were due could be paid. My mother was always very anxious when this happened, but my father would calmly go through the stack of bills, select a few to put aside and then confidently state that "these guys won't go broke if they don't hear from us for a month". My mother would be tearing, or on the verge.

Not that he was so tranquil about every crisis. When a report card came from school listing some problem, or some after school behavior upset our mother, it was her habit to wait until after my father had finished eating dinner before reporting the news. On such occasions anxiety amongst the boys would intensify as dessert was served because we knew that soon, all hell might break loose. Upon hearing the bad news my father was likely to erupt, spew lots of steam and quickly conclude that the problems were the result of too much time spent listening to the radio.

Sometimes this led to the small radio that sat on a table in the living room being sentenced to storage in a closet, with parole being considered when performance or behavior improved. At other times my father would really lose it, and grabbing the radio, he would rush to the cellar, and smash it to smithereens with a hatchet, in spite of pleas from my mother that this solution was insane. After a period without a radio in the living room, my father would arrive home one evening, somewhat sheepishly carrying a cardboard box containing a brand new radio, the exact model and color of the one that had been guillotined. There were at least two episodes when some event involving his children, and whose genesis was attributed by him to the radio, resulted in my father demolishing another radio with his hatchet.

Parents—not to mention the teachers in school—commonly used physical methods to reprimand children's behavior. My mother, who was usually pretty mild tempered, would occasionally take after one of her boys swinging the kitchen broom or—even worse—a hand-held, squid-like contraption with multiple leather tentacles that was known as a "cat and nine tails". This device, which resided on the kitchen door knob, always ready for action, delivered quite a sting. You learned to move quickly. As we grew older, larger and faster, those physical tactics gradually lost their effectiveness.

In contrast to my mother, when my father lost his temper there was no predicting what might follow. When he was a child my father injured his shoulder, leaving it prone to dislocation. On two occasions that I recall, my father, furious with my brother Jim for some transgression, took a swing at Jim and immediately experienced excruciating pain as his arm dislocated from his shoulder joint and dangled listlessly.

Shoring him up as we went, hearing between his moans and groans promises of future repercussions after the shoulder healed, we navigated the four blocks from our house to the emergency room of the Long Island College of Medicine Hospital. While my father lay in pain on a Gurney, a doctor would grab his arm and pull it vigorously away from the chest wall, whereupon it would snap back into the shoulder joint. The arm was then taped and immobilized. Fortunately for my brother Jim, by the time my father recovered weeks later, his furor had pretty much subsided, and combined with the pleas of my mother to avoid having a heart attack, the promised retribution never materialized.

My father's bent for losing his temper may have been an inherited trait. He told us that some time after his mother had died, his oldest brother, my Uncle Ed, had been instructed by my grandfather to purchase a ham and prepare it for the Easter dinner. Ed got distracted on Saturday, and only after the shops had closed did he remember about the ham. In a panic, he went to an uncle of my grandfather, who owned a butcher shop, explained his predicament, and succeeded in getting a ham. For reasons that were never explained, my grandfather and his uncle did not get along, and had not spoken for years. During Easter dinner my grandfather commented on how tasty the ham was, and asked Ed where he had gotten it. When Ed told him that he got it at Uncle Louie's, my grandfather stood up, took the platter with the ham, walked to a rear window of their second story flat, and flung the ham into the back yard.

Hopefully, Irish tempers are learned behaviors and not genetic traits, but from my experience, the evidence is conflicting and inconclusive.

Chapter Three

By the time I was born my parents already had three children, my sisters Muriel and Helen, and my bother Jim. My brother Bill was born about 17 months after me. We lived in a brick row house at 227 Warren Street, where my parents rented the lower two floors. The owners of the house, an immigrant couple from Germany, lived on the upper two floors. They did not have children, were cordial but rather private. The lower of our two floors was slightly below street level and had two rooms, a kitchen and a parlor. All of us slept in two bedrooms on the second floor, where we also shared the single small bathroom. There was an unfinished cellar with a cobble stone floor, where a coal burning furnace heated the house until it was replaced by a oil-burning furnace when I was about 5 years old.

Row houses were connected side to side with no space in between. In front of our house a gated iron railing separated the sidewalk from a sunken concrete airway that stepped down to the doorway to the lower entrance. In the rear of the house there was a very small yard which had a tiny garden plot that was bordered by a rectangular path of flagstones. The combination of surrounding buildings that blocked direct sunlight and soil that appeared to contain mostly inorganic material produced a garden that yielded little botanical life except for some English Ivy that grew up a brick wall at the rear of the yard.

Suspended across the yard were clotheslines where, except on Sundays, my mother hung the laundry to dry. She scrubbed the laundry on a knuckle-thrashing washboard in a large cast iron tub that was fixed to a corner wall in the kitchen, and was covered with a hinged lid of white enameled metal. Until we grew too big to fit into it, the tub was where my brothers and I had our weekly baths on Saturday evenings. On occasion a neighbor arrived at the door in the middle of my bath, but before having them enter the room, my mother—I'm not sure why—would gently push my head down, lower the lid of the tub, and tell me to be quiet while she invited the visitor into the kitchen. I never knew whether the visitor realized that while they spoke with my mother, there was someone in the tub.

For the kids in the neighborhood, the street was our playground. On the sidewalks we played hop-scotch, in the curbside gutters we played several games that used round glass marbles, where a building had a wall without windows, we played handball and games with names like "Geronimo", "Donkey" and "Boxball". Our favorite game was "Fistball", which got its name from the way the ball was hit. The soft, white ball used in fistball was called a "pimple ball" because its surface had numerous tiny elevations, the size and shape of mosquito-bites. The hitter tossed the ball overhead and then punched it either with the closed fist for power, or with the cupped palm to put a spin on the ball so that it took a curved flight. A skilled player could hit what was called a "banana ball", named for the shape of its trajectory. A well-hit banana ball could disappear over rooftops only to reappear still in continuous flight further down the street.

Because of its spin and erratic flight, a banana ball was very difficult to catch on the fly. Each team had six players and the rules were much like baseball, except there were no balls or strikes, because the ball was not pitched. Home plate was a manhole cover (a sewer cover) in the middle of the street, second base was a manhole cover about 120 feet away. First and third bases were boxes drawn with chalk at the curbside pavement half way between home plate and second base. Sliding into a base on the asphalt was tough on your butt and on your pants.

Occasionally, a game was halted by the arrival of a police patrol car responding to a neighbor's complaint about noise, or a ball hitting a window. The police were usually very nice in the way they told us that the game was over, communicating without words their lack of enthusiasm for this aspect of their duties. A few neighbors were rather crabby about fistball games played in front of their houses, and if a ball bounced their way some would grab it and keep it. One particularly nasty old man would cut the ball in half with his pocketknife and throw the two pieces back into the street.

Between gifts received on birthdays and at Christmas, by age ten, most kids owned a pair of roller skates. Each skate consisted of four metal wheels on axles attached to an adjustable metal frame that had to be clamped onto the skater's shoe—sneakers didn't work—and then secured with an ankle strap. Asphalt streets and flagstone sidewalks provided ideal skating surfaces, and hilly streets made for exciting runs all the while dodging autos, pushcarts, pedestrians and stray dogs. A roller skate ride while holding onto the back of a trolley car was a dangerous, hair-raising experience tried once and, except for a few daredevils, never repeated.

When skates no longer fit, they became the essential component of home-made scooters. To each end of a three foot piece of a two-by-four, we nailed a skate and on one end mounted a sturdy, wooden crate, usually rescued from the trash of a vegetable market. Two small slabs of wood were nailed to the top of the crate to serve as handlebars. A small rubber strip, cut from a discarded automobile tire and anchored to the two-by-four with nails, dragged along the pavement as the scooter sped down a hill, but functioned nicely as a break, when the scooter driver stepped on it.

Everyone decorated their scooter,. Some painted them with a mixture of shiny, bright colors, others created designs with hundreds of bottle caps tacked to the front of the wooden crate; everyone nailed foxtails, pennants or colorful streamers to the tips of their handlebars. No one I knew owned a bicycle, primarily because, if you did own one, there would be no place to keep it: small rooms and large families made for cramped living quarters. Nobody had a garage because almost no one had a car.

Summers in Brooklyn sometimes reached extreme levels of discomfort. It was not unusual on hot, humid nights for people to put mattresses on their fire escapes, or their rooftops, and to sleep outdoors. Whether it was from sirens on fire trucks, police cars or ambulances, booming sounds from a juke box in a corner saloon, or loud voices from the sidewalk where Yankee and Dodger fans argued about some baseball statistic, the noises of the street always sounded louder on hot summer nights.

When the days were hot, there were several ways of cooling off. A favorite was to open a "Johnny-pump" (fire hydrant) with a wrench, thereby releasing a torrent of water into the street. Holding a flat piece of wood against the hydrant, it was possible to elevate and broaden the water stream so that it formed a cool shower to play in, right in the middle of the street. When an auto approached, the piece of wood was lowered so as not to douse the occupants, whose windows were always down on hot summer days before air-conditioned cars.

The Johnny-pump showers were periodically interrupted by the arrival of a police car, that in the summer was always equipped with a pipe wrench. After the police turned off the pump and had departed, it would again be opened. This back and forth, between the men in blue and the kids, like a game of ping-pong, would often go on till well after dark.

Another way to cool off was to walk about twenty blocks to a large public swimming pool in Red Hook, where for 7 cents you could spend the entire day. Some of us became skilled in jumping onto the back of the Court Street trolley car where, with bathing suits stuffed in our back pockets, two or three of us at a time could ride to the end of the line, which was very close to the swimming pool. In the early 1940's an epidemic of polio kept the pools from opening, but the closure led to kids swimming off the docks in the waters of New York harbor.

Skinny-dipping in the harbor by jumping off barges moored to the docks at the end of Amity Street was a popular summer recreation for some kids. The large ships that docked there often carried coffee and cocoa from overseas. Their fragrances masked the foul smells of the polluted harbor water. Jumping naked from barges for the first time was a bit scary, and you learned early not to swallow any water.

We weren't smart enough to be concerned about polio, hepatitis and the other health risks of swimming in waters polluted by discharges that spewed from small circular openings in the sides of moored ships, or drained from large orifices of rat-infested storm sewers that fed into the harbor. Sunlight, where it reflected off slicks of oil, produced rainbow sheened puddles on the water's surface. Some days a flaccid condom could be seen idly floating.

Once in the water, getting back up onto the barge for the first time could be a challenge. It required shimmying naked up a thick, scratchy hemp dock line that you made sure was hanging over the side of the barge before jumping into the water. Without the dock line you would have to swim to the storm sewer orifice, and make your way up over slippery rip-rock, an adventure that, fortunately, I never had to experience.

Occasionally, the arrival of a dock security guard required the quick retrieval of clothes and a hasty departure. Once, while running along the dock headed for the street, a guard in hot pursuit -all the while me getting dressed on the fly- I felt the tip of his nightstick in my loins. Never a particularly fast runner, I amazed myself, and my comrades by zipping to the front of the pack, as if my legs had been put in overdrive. We made it over the cyclone fence and didn't stop running for several blocks, by which time the guard had given up the chase.

To any sensible person, it should have been obvious that the water in the harbor was polluted, but, at that age, none of us were smart enough to be concerned about contracting hepatitis or being exposed to the other hazards of swimming in the harbor. I remember once coming to the surface and one of my buddies telling me that a condom was sitting on my shoulder. I carefully looked sideways, confirmed his observation, took a deep breath, slowly descended below the surface, and parted company with what we called a "harbor shark".

Chapter Four

When I was about 9 years old, each day after school, my mother sent me to my grandmother, a few minutes' walk, to see if there were chores or errands that I could do for her. She lived in a small brick rowhouse that had three floors, the lowest being below street level. The house lacked central heating and hot water and had a single bathroom. The kitchen, located on the lower floor, had a coal stove for cooking and heating water, and a walk-in closet that was used as a coal bin. All the rooms in the house were small and had low ceilings. In the winter each of the four bedrooms had a portable electric heater that radiated warmth from a hot, bright orange wire coil set behind a protective screen, and each bed was covered with a thick layer of blankets and quilts. Until my Uncles Richie, Jim, Willie and Eddie, and my Aunt Jean, left for military service in World War II, fourteen Hendersons shared the four bedrooms and a single bathroom.

From my earliest memories of my grandmother, she always seemed old, frail and tired. She walked with a wobbly side-to-side gait and her curved posture made her appear shrunken. The skin on her face was finely wrinkled, and her complexion was pale and sallow. Like many adults of her generation, her cheeks were sunken and her lips retracted, hallmark features of being toothless. I don't think she ever used cosmetics or went to a hairdresser. When her short straight grey hair needed to be cut, this was done by one of her daughters.

As they approached middle age, women of my grandmother's generation developed a constellation of health problems, particularly skeletal, that were the delayed consequences of so many pregnancies and inadequate nutrition. The net effect was that as they aged they became shorter, they stooped over, were prone to hip fractures, and they appeared to be much older than their chronological age.

By nature my grandmother was passive, usually said little, and often seemed to be off in thought somewhere else. Possibly she was thinking about Francis, her second child, who died at 10 months of age from an infection. Or about Mary, her third child, who as an infant suffered a brain injury in a fall from a high chair, and until she died at age 60, spent every day secluded at home, mentally retarded, physically underdeveloped, and emotionally unstable. Possibly she wasn't thinking of anything in particular, but was just worn out from all the years of hardship, since becoming at age 40 a widow with 14 children—one yet to be born—and 8 of them below the age of 15 years.

At the time I was doing errands and chores for my grandmother, all of my aunts and uncles were adults and, except for Mary, were healthy and independent. When I arrived in the afternoons, Grandma was usually bundled in a black shawl sitting where she spent much of her day, next to a window that looked out onto the street, her line of vision at the level of passing ankles. Except for family, the window was her contact with the outside world. Her constant companion was a gentle, black, arthritic cocker spaniel with long curly hair, who moved about the house slowly, and with obvious difficulty.

I never saw my grandmother outside of her house, except on a rare Sunday morning when, with a daughter supporting her on each side, she slowly made her way up Court Street to St. Paul's Church. It could just be my memory, but I can't recall ever seeing her reading a book or a newspaper, or listening to a radio. When she died from heart failure in 1945, she looked so much older than her 61 years. Thinking about her, fifty years after she died, I have no doubts that she was a chronic cardiac cripple, who had severe osteoporosis, a chronic anemia and a longstanding depression.

One of my regular chores was to get fuel for her kitchen stove. Keeping the house warm during the winter required constantly burning something in the kitchen stove. Coal for household consumption was scarce during World War II, because most of the nation's coal was directed to industries that supported the war effort. Whenever word spread through the neighborhood that a barge loaded with coal had entered the Gowanus Canal, long lines of hopeful customers quickly formed outside of the coal yards.

Most of the time her stove burned charcoal that was purchased, and wood that was scavenged. Charcoal was usually available and one of my jobs was to buy bags of it at a local store, and carry them back to my Grandmother's house. My brothers and I were always on the lookout for discarded wood. If we saw crates in the trash outside of a market or a warehouse, or found discarded wooden furniture at a curbside, we hauled it home to be broken into pieces small enough to fit into Grandma's stove. In our cellar there was a chopping block, a three-foot tall log—also the site of radio massacres—on which the wood was chopped with a hatchet, and then later carried to Grandma's house.

One of my weekly errands was to take a shopping bag full of shoes from her house to the local cobbler for repair. With so many aunts and uncles living in the same house, there were always soles and heels that needed resurfacing. The walking surfaces of shoes were made of leather, and the pounding they took from the flagstones and asphalt of New York's streets assured a short lifespan. Rubber was not available during World War II and the long-lasting synthetic materials used today for the bottoms of shoes had not yet been invented.

The neighborhood cobbler shop was owned and operated by the two Spizzano brothers, both bachelors who had immigrated to Brooklyn from Italy. The younger brother did not speak English and worked repairing shoes at the bench, where he supervised several young Italian men, none of whom spoke English, and whose dark complexions reflected their roots in southern Italy. There was a steady turnover of these young men who, sponsored by the Spizzanos, came to the United States, got their start in the shoe repair shop, and then moved on. Sponsoring young people from the old country was a very common pattern amongst Italians and Irish in New York City.

The older Spizzano spoke English and was the front-man of the business. Fashionably dressed and always wearing a white shirt, tie and jacket, he spoke with a heavily accented, gravelly voice that warmly greeted all who entered the shop. He was held in particularly high esteem by Catholics in South Brooklyn because when Cardinal Eugenio Pacelli—who was later to become Pope Pius XII—visited New York City in the late 1930's, he came to Brooklyn to see Mr. Spizzano, his friend from back in Italy.

Living in the cellar of the building where the Spizannos had their shop was a strange man who everyone in the neighborhood knew only as John. I'm not sure that was his real name, but John is what we all knew him by. I never heard anyone mention his last name; I doubt if anybody I knew, even knew it. John was the neighborhood iceman.

The story on John was that he had emigrated from Italy, and as far as anyone in the neighborhood knew, he did not have any family in this country. The entrance to his cellar was through a pair of hinged wooden doors that angled up from the sidewalk to the wall of the building and covered steep, uneven stone steps that descended into darkness below the street. There was nothing—not a number, a mail slot, or a doorbell—that suggested someone lived in the cellar. Set into the sidewalk pavement was a heavy iron disc, which when lifted exposed a chute that led into John's chamber, and onto which a delivery truck driver emptied barrels of coal periodically throughout the winter.

Had you asked children in the neighborhood to describe John in one word, the older ones would have said: "hairy"; the younger ones would have said: "scary".

On hot summer days John, and his dark work clothes were always wet. A haggard figure, he moved about the neighborhood hunched behind a wobbly three-wheeled pushcart, whose handle he grasped with both hands. It seemed to take all of his energy just to keep the cart moving.

Thick black locks hid his brow and temples, dense wiry hairs covered his arms, and spirals from his hairy chest lined the rim of his sweaty undershirt. As he made his way, he usually ignored passersby, but occasionally turned his head their way and expelled some guttural sounds, exposing crooked teeth and the gaps in between. His eyes sat behind bushy eyebrows and jutting cheekbones, and if he did shoot a glance your way, their whites flashed like specks of glitter on a dark hairy mask. Hunched shoulders, short stature, odd sounds, all the hair—subtle mimics of our simian ancestry.

In the pushcart were large slabs of ice covered with layers of wet burlap, old potato sacks discarded by the vegetable market across from his subterranean dwelling. Viewed from the sidewalk as he pushed his cart in the street, the shoes he wore were curved like the rungs of a toy rocking chair. His sockless toes were visible where the tips of each shoe had been cut away, and it appeared from his gait that he walked on his heels.

Arriving at a customer's house, securing the dripping wet cart at the curb, making his way into the front hallway, he would shout a bevy of sounds that his customers seemed to know meant: "Do you want ice?"

Returning to the cart he would pull an ice pick from his belt, cut a block from one of the large slabs, and toss the burlap-wrapped block up on his shoulder. As it dripped cold water onto the back of his shirt, he hugged the block with one arm, and hunched as he went, made his way back to the house, and slowly climbed its stairs. Reaching the customer's kitchen, he put the block into the upright wooden cabinet used to store meat, dairy products, and vegetables in that era before electric refrigerators were common.

In the winter John's cart also carried five-gallon tin drums filled with kerosene. The kerosene was burned in upright floor stoves that heated the rooms in homes lacking central heating. The kerosene-burning stoves were a constant fire hazard and the fumes they emitted gave the rooms a rank odor that was carried to school on children's clothing. If you got near John, be it summer or winter, he smelled of kerosene.

Whenever snow was on the ground, or if it was an unusually cold day, John would tie sheaths of newspaper around his shoes and ankles, presumably to protect his feet.

If you got too near to John, he would snarl aggressively and mutter words in Italian, only a few of which—the obscene ones—we understood. It was as if without knowing you, John didn't like you. When we were very young, my friends and I were afraid of John because of his looks and strange ways, and because of the gossipy tales that were spread about terrible things that went on in his cellar. I'm sure that the stories were totally unfounded.

As a teenager, I hardly saw John, in part because playing basketball and having an after school job took me away from the streets he traversed. On those rare occasions when I saw him moving his pushcart in the street, I felt sorry for him because he seemed so worn, hapless and alone.

On one of my visits home while I was in the Navy, I learned from my father that John had died several years before. Worried when they had not seen him for several days, an unusual occurrence, some concerned neighbors called the police, who entered his cellar and found him dead.

To the amazement of everyone, an article about John appeared in the Brooklyn Eagle after his death and revealed that he had owned several apartment buildings in Brooklyn, and had accumulated substantial sums of money. His estate was inherited by two relatives who lived in Italy.

Why John lived under such miserable conditions all those years remained a mystery.

Chapter Five

From time to time, I've tried to recall my earliest memories. While having some vague recollections of events that occurred earlier, my first vivid memory is, at age five, being at the 1939 World's Fair in New York City with two of my aunts. Around the same time I remember my father pointing to a ship in New York Harbor and saying that it was loaded with scrap metal, and was on its way to Japan. That had to be before September, 1940 when President Franklin Roosevelt, in response to Japan's aggressive military actions throughout the Far Pacific, actions that were the antecedents of World War II, placed an embargo on sending raw materials to Japan.

My father was fascinated by ships; especially the trans-Atlantic passenger liners that came to New York. The office where he worked was near the top of a downtown Manhattan skyscraper and through its windows he could see ships as they moved in and out of New York Harbor. Over the years he became so familiar with each of them that, like an expert birder who identifies spring warblers by their songs, he could identify each liner by the sounds of its horn. Living only four blocks from the waterfront, the noises of the harbor were always in the background. Once in a while a ship's horn would sound in the distance and my father would exclaim that the French liner *Normandie*, the *Queen Mary*, or some other famous ship was passing through the harbor.

Some Sunday afternoons he would take us to Battery Park at the lower tip of Manhattan, where we would board the Staten Island Ferry for a ride across New York Harbor. The fare for the round trip was a nickel. The ferry ride was an exciting adventure for my brothers and me because the harbor was always busy with ships, tug boats, and barges coming and going. Sometimes we would see an aircraft carrier or some other large naval vessel. He showed us how to tell where ships were from by recognizing their national flags. There was a book at home which had the flags of every country, and with time I got to know all of them.

He also showed us many of the city's landmarks that were visible from out on the harbor. One of the easiest to see was the green oxidized copper steeple of St. Paul's Church on Court Street, just around the corner from where we lived. Some Sundays he would take us to the piers along the Hudson River in mid-town Manhattan, the mooring sites of the famous trans-Atlantic passenger liners. Looking up at them from street level, seeing their enormous size, their brightly colored smokestacks, and their graceful lines; touching the gigantic braids of hemp that secured the ships to the massive bollards on the pier, these are images that are as vivid today as the day on the pier. A few years later, on a Sunday afternoon during World War II, we stood at the foot of a pier and looked at the *Normandie,* laying on its side, half sunk, still smoking, destroyed by fire, the victim of sabotage.

On December 7, 1941, the day that Japan attacked Pearl Harbor, my sisters had taken me to a movie. When we returned home our parents told us that the country was at war. I was 7 years old and didn't know what war really meant, except that it was something bad. Many young men, and several young women in the neighborhood, enlisted or were drafted into military service. In the windows of homes small flags with stars appeared: a blue star for each family member in the service, a gold star for a family member killed in action. With the large size of families in our neighborhood it was not uncommon to see flags with three or more stars. My grandmother's window had a flag with five stars.

During the war certain foods and other essential items were in short supply and some were only available sporadically. The government initiated a system of rationing. Every month each household received books of coupons, issued by the government, that could be used to purchase rationed items, when they were available. The size of the family determined how many coupons each household received. There were separate coupons for dairy, meat, coffee, gasoline, tobacco and other items. To make a purchase you needed money and coupons.

When the local butcher let it be known that his shop would soon be receiving a delivery of meat, a long line of customers formed in front of the shop on the day the shipment was expected. The line started to form before the shop opened, even though it was never known at what time the truck with the meat would arrive. When school was not in session my mother would insert me in the line with instructions to keep her place while she left to do other things. Every so often she would return and when the line had moved so that I was near the door of the shop, she would take my place and I would be free to go.

The types and quantity of meats that arrived on the truck were never known in advance, but the sooner you got in line the better the chance you had of getting something you liked. Between deliveries there were days when the butcher shop had only some unusual items such as a hogs head, pig's feet, ox tails, soup bones or tripe, and there were some days when the butcher shop remained closed because there was nothing to sell.

When meat was cooked all the grease was collected in cans where it congealed, and then it was returned to the butcher shop where the customer received cash depending on the weight of the fat. I remember once a person in the neighborhood was caught partially filling the cans with sand and then overlaying it with grease. From that day on the butcher always probed the fat with a knife before weighing it, to be sure that there were no bogus contents.

Some evenings during the war there was excitement because the air raid sirens would be sounded. Whenever this happened all the lights in the city were supposed to be immediately turned off to prevent enemy aircraft from using them as navigation aids. Since it was impossible to function indoors at night without any lights, at the first wail of a siren families scrambled to pull the shades and close the drapes, and to hang blankets intended to make the windows light-proof.

Each street had several volunteer Air Raid Wardens, usually middle-aged men from the neighborhood who appeared to love being in charge. Wearing arm bands and white helmets that displayed the Civil Defense Corps emblem, running up and down the street blowing whistles and shouting orders, they pounded on windows and doors wherever a slit of light could be seen from the street. Most times after the wailing of the sirens ceased, we learned that it had only been a drill; occasionally we learned that an unidentified aircraft had been detected somewhere along the East coast and that the alert was for real.

Many interesting changes took place during World War II. The shortage of oil and gasoline resulted in some businesses reverting from trucks to the use of horse-drawn wagons for making their deliveries. Horse manure became common on the streets, where it complicated roller-skating, fistball games and touch football.

Shortages of certain essential materials triggered episodes of recycling called "scrap drives". Periodically, it was announced that free admission to a major league baseball game would be given to every person who came to the ball park with a designated amount of scrap metal, newspaper or cardboard.

I remember riding in the subway with my father, brothers and neighborhood kids, all of us loaded down with old metal pipes, bundles of newspapers and assorted junk, on our way to Yankee Stadium or the Polo Grounds. Our ragamuffin appearance along with the bundled trash attracted the attention of many subway passengers.

Outside of the stadium there were enormous piles of various materials that steadily grew as fans passed by, pitched their recycled material on the heap, and headed to their free seats in the bleachers.

There wasn't a systematic method used to assure that each fan had brought the proper amount of "scrap": it was basically an honor system. I remember seeing a group of guys arrive carrying a large kitchen stove and another group that brought an enormous hot water boiler tank. From the size of the piles and some of the objects on them, I think the honor system worked, but I remember my father once commenting that an occasional fan "threw a paper clip on the pile", and then walked into the ball-park.

The government encouraged citizens to help ease food shortages and support the war effort by growing some of their own vegetables in what were called "Victory Gardens". While this was feasible for people who lived in the country, it was not very practical for people who lived in places like Warren Street where there was so little tillable ground. Nonetheless, signs of some agricultural efforts appeared in our neighborhood.

People grew tomato plants and some vegetables in pots or in boxes on their roofs and fire escapes. A few families who lived in apartment buildings with large cellars began to keep chickens. Although it was against public health regulations to house chickens in domestic dwellings, for a few years the early morning crowing of roosters was a common sound in our neighborhood.

During the summer when I was nine years old, my brother Bill and I got the idea to plant a "Victory Garden" in the tiny yard at the back of our house. With a hoe we chopped and turned over the ground and then cut and buried some potatoes that had sprouted small tubers during storage in the kitchen pantry. We diligently watered our garden and became very excited the day we first saw tiny sprouts emerging from cracks in the soil directly over where we had planted the pieces of potato.

With time we had plants growing in the middle of the yard and some of them reached a size where we had to prop them with sticks to keep them from laying on the ground. The plants seemed to be very healthy and we continued to water them regularly, but potatoes never appeared. We waited and waited, but they never came. As the summer progressed we began to lose interest and decided that the ground was not rich enough to yield a crop, a prediction we had heard from others when we first talked about planting a Victory Garden. By the end of the summer all of the plants had died.

The following year we decided to try again. We sliced some sprouting potatoes and as we began to dig the ground to plant them, we found numerous rotten potatoes buried in the soil.

It will probably be very difficult for you to believe this, but Bill and I did not know that the potatoes on a potato plant were located under the ground, and not on the plant above the ground. All that previous summer we had been waiting for the potatoes to appear on the plants, not knowing that we had to dig them out of the ground. Until this day I can not explain why some adult did not tell us where to look. Over the years whenever I told others about our Victory Garden, they find it hard to believe that it is a true story. One witty listener proposed that the adults actually didn't know where the potatoes were, and this might explain the Great Potato Famine that occurred in Ireland during the 19th century.

When the news arrived that the War had ended there was tremendous excitement and jubilation. The streets quickly filled with people celebrating and cheering, hugging and crying. Horns blew, sirens wailed, church bells rang, saloons served free beer out on the sidewalks, confetti rained from above, and American flags were everywhere. On ordinary days sidewalks belonged to people and streets belonged to vehicles; on the day that the war ended, people spontaneously took over the streets.

From windowsills throughout the neighborhood radios blasted the latest news and the proclamations and speeches from public figures. Our neighborhood was one big street party that lasted into the early hours of the next morning. Once darkness arrived bright beams of light from powerful searchlights crisscrossed the nighttime sky; this time celebrating, not searching for intruders.

Chapter Six

Our neighborhood was an exciting and interesting place to live. It had such a tremendous mixture of everything: people, languages, music, dress, food and aromas. Just on the single block of Warren Street where we lived, there were Irish, Italian, Syrian, African, French, Norwegian, Puerto Rican, Armenian and German families. Except for the Irish and African families, the adults in these families were immigrants to the United States. In the surrounding streets there were families that came from Cuba, Barbados, Spain, Lebanon, Poland, and Greece. Scattered throughout the neighborhood were several small Chinese laundries.

Depending on the wind direction, our neighborhood enjoyed the wonderful aromas of cocoa and coffee being off-loaded from ships along the Brooklyn waterfront, the less wonderful odors of fish from the Fulton Market in lower Manhattan, or the stench from pig farms near Secaucus, New Jersey. The best smells came from the ethnic kitchens in neighborhood homes and nearby restaurants. A trip along Court Street and Atlantic Avenue provided a wonderful assortment of aromas coming from the Italian and Syrian markets where for a few coins you could enjoy great Italian ices, fresh pistachio nuts and chewy strips of dried apricots that we called "shoe leather".

Large families were common in the neighborhood. One family had 19 living children, and several other families had 14 or more children. Italian, Irish, Puerto Rican and African families made up the majority of the neighborhood population. There were quite a few families from Lebanon and Syria. Within a short walk there were many churches: Roman Catholic, Eastern Rite Catholic, Methodist, Calvinist, Greek Orthodox, Episcopal, Evangelical, Quaker and Presbyterian. A small Synagogue was located three blocks from our house.

On a walk through the neighborhood on a Saturday afternoon you might hear Italian opera, Cuban rumbas, Danny Boy or Arabic music coming through open windows, behind which 78-rpm records spinning on hand-cranked Victrolas generated the sounds.

Up on rooftops, old, Italian men could be seen exercising their homing pigeons. Pointing a long pole skyward, strips of ribbon attached to its end like tails on a kite, sketching ellipses in the sky like a conductor with a giant baton, they directed the flight of the pigeons. There were sporting clubs for people who raised pigeons, and periodically a homing pigeon competition took place. Owners paid a fee for each bird they entered in the event. The birds were banded, driven to somewhere in New Jersey or Pennsylvania, and then released. The owner of the first bird to return was awarded all the entry fees.

About a fifteen minute walk from our house stood a twenty five story office building. When the lobby attendant was not present, it was possible to take an elevator to a floor near the top, find a men's room with windows facing west, and look out on New York harbor. On a clear day the view of the Manhattan skyline and the bridges that spanned the East River connecting Brooklyn and Manhattan was spectacular.

Every day except Sunday, the German bakeries in the neighborhood made fabulous cookies, chocolate layer cakes, iced stollens packed with dried fruits and nuts, and custard-filled tarts. The aroma of bread fresh out of the oven at the Italian bakery and its taste when sliced and filled with meatballs and tomato sauce were treats that I loved, but did not fully appreciate how wonderful they were until after I had left home. The Italian pizzerias served only one kind of pizza: thin crust, lots of sauce and mozzarella, a touch of oil and oregano—and wonderful.

Some summer days you might come across an elderly Italian organ grinder who produced music by cranking the organ handle while his small monkey, attached to the organ by a leash, worked the crowd. With cup in hand the monkey would scamper up to anybody who stopped, expectantly shaking the cup. Whenever he was successful, which was quite often, the monkey would dart back to the organ grinder who took the coin and, while continuing to crank out the tune, acknowledged the donor with a nod of the head and a smile.

Up until the time I left home in 1952, I never saw a pizza cross our doorsill. My father was a very old fashioned, meat and potatoes Irishman, and to say that he lacked culinary curiosity would be a gross understatement. After his mother died and until he married, my father lived in households, in which all meals were prepared by Irish bachelors, probably accounting at least in part for his restricted tastes. I am pretty sure that a slice of pizza never crossed his lips, nor did he ever eat any Chinese or Mexican food. Ethnic food was a Nathan's hot dog. Simply mentioning the words garlic or chili pepper gave him indigestion.

I think my mother had a somewhat more adventuresome appetite because she would often prepare side dishes that she would eat in advance of the meal: what was put on the table reflected my father's tastes. In a neighborhood that was a literal melting pot, most families stuck pretty close to the dietary customs and music tastes of their ancestors, a tradition that made me wish I was Italian.

"Stick with your own kind!"

That was an admonition I heard many times. Sometimes it came from a nun or priest, sometimes from a relative, sometimes from a neighbor. Coming from nuns and priests, "your own kind" meant Catholics; coming from relatives it meant Irish, or at the outer limit, whites. Delivered without loathing or contempt for the excluded ones, the warnings were like the taboos of a primitive people, unquestioned sacred truths.

Some ethnocentric behavior defied reality and bordered on the humorous. The family of my teammate Eddie had one of the first television sets in the neighborhood. Hinting for an invitation to watch a Brooklyn Dodger game on T.V., I was warned by Eddie that his father did not permit any talking while watching a game. This was an extension to baseball watching, of his policy at the dining room table during meals.

Eddie's father was a rigidly opinionated, immigrant Irishman who spoke with a strong brogue. One afternoon while we were watching a game, Eddie's father became annoyed by loud Arabic music that was coming from the adjacent apartment. He banged on the wall with his fist and yelled to turn down the volume. He did this several times without any effect. In his thick Irish accent he started ranting about "the goddamn foreigners" on the other side of the wall.

Reaching the point of exasperation, jumping up from his chair, grabbing his walking stick, leaning out the front window of his apartment, he began rapping his stick on the window of his Middle Eastern neighbors. Then, there was the sound of broken glass. I doubt that he intended to break the window, but the combination of his incensed energy and a hefty walking stick were too much for the pane of glass.

Hastily retreating to his chair, he continued to mutter about the foreigners, seemingly oblivious to his immigrant past, while the music next door continued unabated.

From time to time a band of gypsies would arrive in the neighborhood, an event that always triggered excitement and gossip. Moving into a vacant store, covering the windows with brightly colored sheets of cloth, the group would stay for a few weeks, or a few months, and then one day would be gone.

Peeking into their store, it was not obvious where everyone slept because there was very little furniture. If you walked passed the store at night the dim lights within created in the windows a reddish-purple screen upon which were projected the shadows of human movements. Considering the size of the store and the number of people—mostly women and children—living inside, the conditions were very crowded.

The gypsy women wore bright clothes and head-cloths, used a lot of makeup and some of them wore large earrings. Their children did not attend school. Adult gypsies had little interaction with their neighbors. Although from time to time a sign advertising fortune-telling appeared in the window, I never knew of anyone who ventured in to learn what their future held.

Children in the neighborhood were intrigued by gypsies because of their exotic dress and mysterious behavior. Adults in the neighborhood were typically prejudiced, suspicious and even fearful. Our parents warned us to stay clear of gypsies, even if they appeared to be friendly. Although the gypsies did not seem to be particularly well off, occasionally some gypsy men would arrive at the store in a fancy, polished, brightly colored Cadillac convertible. Whenever this happened, the neighborhood gossip held that there had been a visit from a "gypsy king".

Our neighborhood had three small movie theatres. Children's admission was 11 cents on Saturdays and 14 cents on Sundays. Each theatre showed two full-length movies, a chapter of a serial western, a cartoon, a newsreel and previews of the coming attractions. The films were almost always in black and white, and the program changed each week. Unlike movie theatres of today, there were no intermissions and no advertisement on the screen. The program was shown continuously from when the theatre opened about noon until it closed that night. Viewers commonly arrived after a movie had already begun. Taking their seats during a scene in the middle of the movie, they stayed through the next showing until that scene again appeared, at which point they would exit the theatre. On rainy days, or when a movie was outstanding, it was not unusual for some viewers to stay and see the movie a second time. Occasionally, a movie had such a surprise ending, admittance was not allowed during the final ten or fifteen minutes.

While movies were being shown, an old man walked the aisles selling candy, pop corn and soda from a large basket. Each theatre employed a woman, usually short, large and tough: she was called a "matron". She patrolled the aisles wearing a white smock and carrying a flashlight that would send a beam of light your way if she suspected shenanigans, or saw your arm around the girl in the next seat. Necking was not permitted; if you wanted to neck you had to go to a theatre that had a balcony.

In retrospect, it seems unbelievable but smoking was permitted in movie theatres. Certain rows were designated as the smoking section; the smokers were separated from the non-smokers but the smoke was not.

One of the most interesting places in our neighborhood was a tiny shop, about eight feet wide and twenty feet deep that was operated by a man named Maxie Korn. He and his wife were immigrant Polish Jews who put in 15 hour days, 7 days a week, and had tiny living quarters at the back of the shop. They sold cigarettes, cigars, candy, soda pop, "pimple balls", an amazing inventory of comic books, and newspapers of several languages including a popular "tip sheet" called The Armstrong Daily, which handicapped horses running at race tracks in the New York City area.

Maxie's was a busy place: it had the only public telephone booth in the neighborhood and—even though it was illegal—at Maxie's a teenager could buy single cigarettes—called "loosies"—for a penny a piece. The purchase was essentially an under-the-counter operation. You could not select a particular brand, the loosies you got came from whatever pack Maxie happened to have open, usually one of his slowest moving brands.

Unfortunately, many youngsters -mostly boys- began smoking when they were 12 or 13.

This was an era when cigarette ads showed athletes, physicians and movie stars smoking and attesting to the quality and enjoyment of particular brands. At Ebbets Field, the home of the Brooklyn Dodgers, whenever a player hit a home run, he was given a complimentary carton of Old Gold cigarettes, the sponsor of the radio broadcasts. From his booth suspended beneath the upper grandstands behind home plate, each time a home run was hit, Red Barber, the voice of the Dodgers, pitched the carton of Old Golds onto the foul ball screen, and the carton tumbled down to field level where it was retrieved by the team's batboy and presented to the slugger.

I had just turned thirteen when I smoked my first cigarette: I continued to smoke for about another forty years. My brothers, Jim and Bill, and my sisters, Muriel and Helen were early smokers, although none of us were allowed to smoke at home until we were 18. My mother regularly warned us that in addition to making us and our clothing smell foul, cigarette smoking was harmful because it stunted your growth.

The real health hazards of smoking were not widely appreciated or acknowledged in the United States at that time, even though studies in Scandinavian countries had already shown that cigarette smokers had an increased risk of developing heart disease and lung cancer. The diseases caused by cigarette smoking belong to a category of diseases that I have taught students can be considered as "time-bomb diseases": the diseases become manifest only after decades of apparent good health. During this asymptomatic period—when to the smoker the habit seems to be harmless—insidious cellular and tissue injury is continuously occurring, perpetrated by chemicals contained in tobacco smoke: then one day the disease announces its presence.

While tobacco leads to heart disease in adults, heart disease in children, which was not uncommon in our neighborhood, has other causes. In that era before antibiotics, epidemics of rheumatic fever and diphtheria were serious public health problems, particularly in large cities. Both diseases present as severe sore throats and are caused by bacteria that are readily spread from person to person, especially amongst people living in crowded conditions.

In diphtheria the bacteria are present in the throat, not in the heart, but toxins made by the bacteria enter the blood, reach the heart and cause serious cardiac injury. In rheumatic fever the patient's immune system makes antibodies in an attempt to eradicate the bacteria. This strategy is usually effective, but unfortunately, certain molecules in our heart are structurally similar to some of the molecules produced by the bacteria: the net effect is that some of the antibodies directed to the bacterial molecules also react with molecules in the heart where the inflammation they cause results in serious cardiac injury.

One of my friends died from rheumatic fever when he was twelve years old. Had penicillin been available then, he would have been treated and survived. My brother Jim spent the best part of a summer in bed with rheumatic fever, but fortunately recovered. Another important cause of heart disease in children is birth defects. At the time I was a child the most serious heart defects resulted in death at birth, or early in infancy. Less severe defects allowed survival into the teens when death resulted from heart failure. Today, virtually all of those heart defects would be diagnosed at birth, or soon thereafter, and would be successfully corrected with surgery.

There were many other diseases seen in children then that are much less common now. My best friend's sister spent years of her childhood in a tuberculosis sanitarium. There were several children in our neighborhood who were confined to wheel chairs because of severe cerebral palsy, a consequence of brain injury during birth, or because of polio. While cerebral palsy still occurs in this country, its frequency is greatly reduced because of improved prenatal and obstetric care. It was not uncommon to see children with Downs' Syndrome.

Because of my brother Brian, I was aware of Down's and remember seeing Down's children on the street, often in the company of an older woman, presumably their grandmother. In medical school I learned that Down's is a disorder that occurs in children born to older mothers, usually forty or more years of age. So the elderly women I had seen were most likely the mothers of the child, not the grandmothers. It is now known that eggs as they develop in old ovaries are prone to make mistakes when the chromosomes are replicated and then separated. Instead of each egg having one copy of the 23 human chromosomes, some eggs in old ovaries end up with an extra copy of chromosome #22, a condition termed trisomy 22 which is the basis of Down's Syndrome.

Some diseases that previously were common are now much less common because preventive measures have been so effective. A good example is tooth decay. Prior to fluoridation of drinking water, tooth decay and toothaches were extremely common.

When my father was a youngster, dentists often made the rounds of city neighborhoods in horse-drawn wagons searching for business. When a patient with a toothache was found, the dental work would be performed in a chair, up in the wagon. The event usually attracted spectators who watched from the sidewalk, while the dentist extracted the rotten, painful tooth from the terrified patient. Printed in large, bold letters on both sides of the wagon that came to my father's neighborhood were the words: *Painless Parker.*

Dentistry had greatly advanced by the time I was a child: dentists now worked in offices and clinics. When I had a toothache at night, my mother would take a skillet, pour in a cup of table salt, and light a fire under it on the stove. When the sizzling salt grains got so hot that they began to dance in the skillet, she would pour the salt into a stocking and place it on my face, over the aching tooth. This remedy actually gave some relief from the toothache, but I believe this was achieved by *distraction therapy*: the pain from the hot salt on my face distracted me from the pain in my tooth.

Having to have a tooth extracted was like something out of a nightmare. Until I was about ten my mother would take me to the dental clinic at the Long Island College Hospital where for twenty five cents your bad tooth would be attended to by a dental student. When I was about eleven I was sent home from grade school one day with a severe toothache. Upon arrival my mother phoned a dentist and he told her to send me to his office. The dentist's office, one floor above a saloon, was located two blocks from our home. It had a tiny waiting room, a room with a single dental chair, and a small laboratory in the rear where dental prostheses were made.

As he worked in my mouth, there were momentary interruptions as a technician appeared, prosthesis in-the-making in hand, seeking an evaluation of the piece, and further instructions.

Using a shiny set of pliers he made several attempts to extract my tooth, but it did not budge from its attachment to my jaw. From a maze of instruments suspended over the chair, each connected by wires, wheels and swiveling arms to small motors, he pulled down a tool that I soon realized functioned like a miniature pile driver. As it delivered rapid, repetitive, blows to my tooth, producing with each rap the sound of stone on marble, it transferred the thrust of each blow to my jaw which vibrated in synchrony.

Returning to the shiny pliers, the dentist grasped the tooth and pulled, but what came was only the separated crown, leaving behind the roots, which remained firmly anchored in my mandible. At this point the dentist decided that the situation called for the skills of an oral surgeon. He packed one side of my mouth with medicated gauze and cotton cylinders, made some phone calls, took me down to the street where he hailed a taxi, and putting me into it, gave the cabbie instructions and some money.

As the cab made its way through downtown Brooklyn, I was frightened because I had heard the word surgeon and had no idea of what was in store for me. When the cab arrived at the Williamsburg Savings Building, Brooklyn's landmark skyscraper, I was whisked into an elevator, taken to a large dental suite on one of the upper floors, and put into a dental chair that was much fancier than the one I had left fifteen minutes before. The oral surgeon told me that he was going to put a mask over my face and that I had to take deep breaths. The last thing I remembered—before the nitrous oxide from the mask took effect—was seeing a pretty nurse smiling down at me as she took my hand in hers. It was a nice feeling.

When I awoke, I was laying on a couch in another room: the pain was gone, the tooth was gone and the pretty nurse was gone.

Chapter Seven

When I was 6, my parents enrolled me in St. Paul's Elementary School which was located about 50 yards down the street from our house. Living this close had the advantage of being less than a minute's dash away each morning, but had the disadvantage of assuring frequent contacts between my teachers and parents.

Except for two lay instructors, the teachers were nuns of the Order of the Sisters of Charity. Most of the nuns were of Irish descent, and when not in the classroom they lived simple, convent secluded, religious lives. Education at St. Paul's was a process in which students memorized and naively accepted whatever information was presented. Lessons in non-interpretive subjects such as reading, writing, spelling, arithmetic and geography involved rote learning and repetitive drills. Inherently interpretable subjects, such as history, social studies, art and music, were taught using material chosen, presented and interpreted to rigidly instill the dogma and views of the Catholic Church. There was only one way to look at things and this had been figured out centuries ago by saints, popes and bishops: open discussions, objective analyses and consideration of alternative views were unheard of.

Most of the teachers were strict authoritarians who created a classroom atmosphere in which order was rigidly controlled. When prolonged standing in a corner of the classroom facing the wall, being kept for an hour or so after school, or being sent to the principal's office proved ineffective, some teachers resorted to physical methods to enforce behavioral compliance.

The school day began with the Pledge of Allegiance and throughout the day there were regular periods devoted to prayer. Every day there were formal lessons in religion, essentially the presentation and justification of Catholic dogma, usually taught by nuns, but sometimes by a priest. The children attending St. Paul's were taught about a vengeful God who monitored your every thought and action, rated the severity of all your transgressions, kept score, and would deal with you in the next world.

Students at St. Paul's were there to be indoctrinated. They were constantly reminded that if they died before confessing their sins to a priest—if the sins were serious enough—they would spend all of eternity burning in hell. We were taught that only people baptized in the Catholic Church could ever get into heaven. If you were not baptized, but led a decent life, when you died you went to a place called Limbo, where you didn't burn, but stayed forever, never to gain entry into heaven. Religious education was an unremitting program aimed at implanting in the students' psyche a set of lifelong behaviors, attitudes and beliefs that would be self-enforced by fear and guilt.

During class students were expected to remain still in their seats, to look straight ahead, and to speak only when called upon or, if they raised a hand, after being recognized by the teacher. My fifth grade teacher, a lay person, had a reputation for being physical in dealing with boys. A regular punishment was vigorous strokes with a blackboard pointer or a ruler delivered across the shoulders or the opened palms of outstretched hands.

This teacher also had the habit of punishing boys—not girls—by having them sit on the floor in the well under her desk. While sitting in her chair at the desk and continuing with the lesson, she would kick the boy whenever he moved or giggled. At that age, none of us were yet savvy to the sexual connotations inherent in such behavior, usually having had no prior experience being so close to legs dangling from a skirt.

Generally, boys were more refractory than girls to belittlement and criticism delivered in front of classmates. When berated by a teacher some girls would lose self-control, and become hysterical. Verbal hounding of an easily intimidated student, publicly humiliating her to the point of tears was a distressing scene to witness.

An event that took place when I was in 4th grade made me realize how culturally isolated and insensitive the nuns were. A Puerto Rican family moved into our neighborhood during the summer of 1944 and on the first day of school in September, the mother enrolled her son in St. Paul's School. The boy, who was called Heyzeus, joined our class but after about a week he stopped coming to school. We later learned from our fourth grade teacher that the boy's name was spelled Jesus. The principal of St. Paul's told the mother that it was a sacrilege for anyone to have the name Jesus, and that the boy's name had to be changed. The family refused and withdrew their son.

Some students struggled academically because their parents did not speak English, and help at home with school assignments was not a realistic possibility. Other students had problems because they came from homes where abuse, chronic alcoholism, poverty or a dysfunctional family structure undermined normal childhood development. It seemed that in dealing with these students teachers were ignorant or insensitive to the underlying circumstances that handicapped performance.

One of my best friends was a classmate who had difficulty learning, had a severe stuttering problem and became easily flustered when called upon in class. On cold winter afternoons we would sometimes go to the flat where he lived and his mother would serve us hot tea. Sometimes his mother had a black eye.

His parents were immigrants from Ireland: his mother a tiny, shy, simple woman who was very religious; his father a belligerent, strapping alcoholic who worked as a stevedore on the Brooklyn docks until drinking led to the loss of his job, and a life of drifting from one menial part-time job to another. He was loathsomeness incarnated.

Mean-spirited, angry and hypercritical, at home he accounted to nobody for his behavior, and his words were unchallenged law. Once while I was there, he shuffled into the kitchen, obviously hung over, muttered some words, and to the great embarrassment of his wife, unzipped his pants, urinated into the sink, and then dragged himself back to bed.

It was obvious that abuse was rampant in that household: the neighbors knew about it, the parish priests knew about it, the police knew about it, but nothing was ever done about it.

In eighth grade the nun who was our teacher told the class an extraordinarily bizarre tale. She was instructing us about *transubstantiation*, the Catholic belief that when a priest blesses the communion bread at mass, the bread is changed into the body of Christ. The nun told us about an elderly, Jewish man who operated a shop that sold newspapers, tobacco and candy, and who was skeptical about this belief held by Catholics. He went to a nearby Church where he surreptitiously received the communion. He quickly returned to his shop where he placed the wafer on a table and stabbed it with a knife. At once blood began flowing from the bread. While not naming names, one could not help but wonder whether she was talking about Maxie.

The nuns regularly reminded us that it was Jews who had crucified Jesus. One nun told us a story about a Chinese laundryman who purposely inoculated the shirt collar of a priest to cause him to get leprosy.

These strange stories were components of a relentlessly parochial curriculum that promoted suspicion and wariness of non-Catholics. The nuns and priests regularly warned of the dangers "to your faith" that came from socializing with non-Catholics, because they would try to convert you to their religion. We were constantly reminded of the risks to "our soul" that came from reading books or seeing movies that had not been approved by the "Legion of Decency" of the Catholic Church. A persistent theme from the first to the eighth grade was that Catholicism was the only "true religion". It was as if, without anyone ever consulting you, forces that knew best had arranged for your salvation, and it was your obligation to unquestionably follow their prescriptions or face dire consequences. I must say that all the religious rigmarole did not interfere with most students acquiring solid foundations in the three R's.

At age 10 I became an altar boy at St. Paul's Church. Parents and nuns encouraged the boys at St. Paul's to become altar boys or choir boys: there was no such thing as an altar girl or a choir girl. The job of an altar boy was to assist the priests in ceremonies such as masses, funerals and weddings. The priests gave us Latin lessons each week where we memorized and learned to pronounce the Latin responses to the prayers they spoke during the services. Brooklynese Latin: it must have interesting to hear. Rarely did any of us know the English translation of the Latin words that we spoke.

Religious ceremonies were conducted in the sanctuary, an area of the church that contained the altar, and which was separated from the congregation by a thick wooden railing. With two exceptions, females were not permitted to enter the sanctuary. One exception was for a few women in the parish who entered weekly to clean the altar, change the linens, dust and polish the furniture, vacuum the rugs, scrub the floors and arrange the flowers. The women who were selected to perform these chores considered it a special honor to be allowed to enter the sanctuary.

The only other time that a woman was allowed to enter the sanctuary was as a bride or a bridesmaid during a marriage ceremony. The exclusion of women from the sanctuary, and consequently from their active participation in religious ceremonies, was particularly ironic, not only because of the cynical exception made to perform janitorial work, but because, by far, the majority of adults who attended church services—and dropped money into the collection basket—were women.

Throughout the church statues of saints and other religious figures sat on pedestals, usually with racks of burning candles in front of them. Parishioners would put coins into the box attached to the rack, then light a candle and pray. It was not uncommon to see an elderly person, usually a woman, on her knees, tears streaming down her face and speaking, in Italian or another foreign language, to one of the statues. Some statues had dollar bills tucked into the spaces between the fingers and the toes, placed there by patrons of that particular saint.

My mother was a very devout Catholic who regularly lit candles and prayed for a miracle that would help my brother Brian develop normally. The only time in her life she traveled outside of the United States was when my sister Muriel drove her, my father and Brian to a Saint's shrine in Quebec, a place where Catholics believed miracles sometimes occurred.

When I was about twelve years old the priest in charge appointed me to be the head altar-boy at St. Paul's Church. My mother was very happy about this because, like many Irish mothers then, she had hopes that one of her sons would someday become a priest, and she was beginning to think that it might be me. One of the benefits of being the head altar-boy was being assigned to assist at weddings and funerals. The Best Man in the bridal party almost always tipped the two altar-boys as much as five dollars each, a lot of money at that time.

Funeral masses were always scheduled for mid-morning on a weekday, which meant that the altar-boys were excused from school for a couple of hours. An additional bonus was a small tip from the Funeral Director, coins which were spent at Maxie's on the way back to school.

The sexton in the church was Mr. Mike Garrihan, an old fellow who spoke with an Irish brogue, had a longtime affair with the spirits, and was not above reaching into the sacristy storeroom, grabbing a bottle of communion wine, and taking a swig. Mike's drinking interfered with getting his chores done, so he gave me a set of church keys, and taught me to ring the steeple bells, to mop the aisles, to lock up the church after the last evening service, and to pass the collection basket at services. He would slip me a dollar or two each week for helping out.

For about a year I was the altar-boy for the daily mass at 6:30 a.m., something that strains imagination considering the Lynch talent for deep sleep. Many days I opened the church because Mike was not there when I arrived. Ringing the church bells was exciting because of the booming sounds the bells made inside of the tower. Three large bronze bells were located high in the steeple and when they tolled, their sounds resounded throughout downtown Brooklyn.

From the clapper of each bell, a thick hemp rope descended about thirty feet to the ringer's platform. It took a mighty pull on each rope to make the clapper strike the bell. I soon found that, instead of just standing on the platform, it worked better for me to jump up, grasp the rope and let the momentum of my descending body cause the clapper to strike the bell. The frequency, spacing and order in which each bell was rung were fixed by religious ritual. Some people, including my mother, claimed that from the cadence and rhythm of the tolling bells, they could tell that it was me in the steeple.

After eight years in St. Paul's Elementary School, it came time for high school. My parents pressured me to attend Bishop Loughlin Memorial, a Catholic high school for boys. My brother Jim had enrolled at Loughlin, but had left after a year. Jim was a bright fellow who later graduated from college, but at age 14 the dogmatic, arrogant atmosphere imposed by the Christian Brothers was not to his liking.

Most of my friends from elementary school were headed for public high-schools, which was where I wanted to go, but my parents prevailed. One year after I started, my brother Bill was also pressured into attending Loughlin, but after one year, he had to leave. Bill later earned a Ph.D. in English at the University of Pennsylvania, and became a college professor. As a teenager, he found the atmosphere of the Catholic high school stifling, and considered the Christian Brothers ecclesiastical thugs.

As a high school teen, I was more interested in sports, girls and hanging out with friends than in studying, or being an altar-boy. These changing priorities reflected hormones, social growth, and pubertal challenge to authority. Intellectually, I had already begun to distance myself from the religious traditions of my family. Having observed priests up close during my years as an altar-boy fostered skepticism about their reverent status.

I was totally turned off by the parochialism at Bishop Loughlin, and put little effort into class work. My attitude and performance generated numerous communications between the Assistant Principal and my mother, renewing an acquaintance begun when my brothers attended Loughlin. She was distraught at the possibility that not one of her sons would graduate from a Catholic High School.

In sophomore year I had to repeat one semester because I failed three subjects. In junior year I switched from the pre-college curriculum to the much easier commercial curriculum. By senior year I had reached a phase of total disinterest in school. Many days I left home in the morning headed for school, but decided instead to explore the city. If it was cold or rainy, the day was spent taking in a triple feature at a 42nd Street movie house. A favorite destination was the Paramount Theatre in Times Square where, in addition to a movie, there was a stage show that featured big bands like Les Brown, Gene Krupa and Lionel Hampton.

On days when I showed up at school, a lot of time was spent sleeping in class. With one exception, this did not seem to bother the teachers. From time to time, seeing that I was out of it, a teacher would direct a question to me, a classmate would tap me on the shoulder, I would look up not knowing what was going on, and then there might be a humorous comment by the teacher, followed by some laughter.

The exception was my homeroom teacher, a Christian Brother who was a blend of arrogance and condescension, and with whom I had a poor relationship. Annoyed and concerned by all the sleeping, he sent me to be evaluated by the school psychologist. I never knew for sure, but I thought that the Brother suspected my sleeping was related to some illicit activity in my neighborhood.

The Brother had an elderly aunt who lived in our neighborhood. I knew he had a poor opinion of the neighborhood, because I had heard him express it to some other Brothers. Possibly he formed this opinion because on visits to his aunt, he had to climb the urine-impregnated stairs of the Warren Street Subway exit, stairs that were always dark because light bulbs were rarely replaced, stairs where newspaper, glass and other trash accumulated, stairs where one might encounter a sleeping wino.

Possibly, it was because, when he reached the top of the stairs, he found himself on a noisy street corner crowded with grubby teenage boys engaged in frivolous Babel. Sometimes I was one of them.

Possibly, it was because in walking the few blocks from the Subway to his aunt's house, he encountered behavior, language and street characters that would never be tolerated at Bishop Loughlin Memorial High School.

After a number of meetings with the psychologist, who was also a Christian Brother, and after exploring many possibilities, he decided that my sleeping was due to staying up late at night, and to smoking cigarettes.

After four and a half years, it came time to graduate, but I didn't have enough credits: I was three courses short. I went to the principle and explained that my mother was telling everyone in the neighborhood that, at last, one of her sons was going to graduate from a Catholic high school. I mentioned that my Aunt Lillie had been bragging to all the nuns in her convent that a Lynch boy was actually going to graduate from Bishop Loughlin.

The principal told me that I needed to go to summer school to make up the coursework in order to receive a diploma. I was relieved when he explained that at the graduation ceremony each student walked across the stage and received a blank piece of paper. Those students who had satisfied all requirements received the actual diploma in the mail; those students who had encumbrances received their diploma after all requirements had been satisfied. I would get a diploma if I went to summer school and passed the three courses. I walked across the stage, my mother was proud, my aunt was pleased, and I felt like I had dodged a bullet.

I couldn't conceive of spending any more time in a classroom, so I did not go to summer school. Instead, I took a job as a counselor at a boy's camp. It was not until four years later, when I was in the Navy, on a ship in the Pacific Ocean, that I took an exam and received a General Equivalency High School Diploma.

My mother and aunt had so much emotion invested in my graduating from Bishop Loughlin, that I never had the heart to crush their pride: they both left this world never knowing any of these details.

Chapter Eight

At age 14, playing basketball became my passion. It started at P.S. 29, a few blocks from our house, and across the street from the house where Winston Churchill's mother was born. On pleasant days my friends and I played outdoors in the schoolyard, on rainy or cold days, we played in the gym. Before long about 10 of us decided to form a team that we named the Cheyennes, and began to play at the Warren Street Community Center. This turned out to be a momentous decision because it introduced me to the Center's director, a man everyone knew as "Smith", a man who would become a mentor and lifelong friend, a man who would profoundly influence the rest of my life.

Henry Clay Smith was a tall, silver haired, broad shouldered, muscular man. Handsome and the picture of health, he was outgoing, had a bounce to his step, and a ready smile. The crowds and sounds of the inner city streets of Brooklyn, where horns and sirens blared, trolley cars screeched and rattled, and subway cars rumbled in the tunnels below, were about as different as it could get from Freeville, New York, the small, rural village near Ithaca, where Smith grew up.

He graduated from Cornell University with a degree in Agriculture just as World War I was underway. After serving in the Army, he moved to Baton Rouge, Louisiana to work for the Southern Pacific Railroad as an agricultural advisor. The railroad owned vast parcels of tillable land along their right-of-ways, acreages that were farmed for the railroad by sharecroppers. His contact with tenant farmers in the rural South brought him face-to-face with the stifling effects of poverty and poor education.

After working in Louisiana for more than ten years, he came to New York City to attend New York University, with the goal of becoming a social worker. During the many years that I knew him, he never spoke about why he left Louisiana, except for an occasional hint about problems he had encountered with the political machine of Louisiana's infamous Governor, Huey Long. Anybody who spent much time around Smith soon appreciated that he was driven by strong egalitarian principles, and that he spoke his mind. These traits and his departure from Louisiana, I have no doubt, were in some way connected.

When he arrived in New York, the country was still in the midst of The Great Depression. He found a job as a custodian in a Methodist Church on Warren Street. In return for looking after the church property, he received a small salary and rent-free space in two rooms of the adjacent parsonage. The job was a good fit for a student: the hours were flexible and it was a short subway ride to classes at NYU.

The Methodist Church on Warren Street was a landmark institution in Brooklyn. For decades it had a large, active congregation, and its rich history reached far back into the 1800s. By the time that Smith became its custodian, things had drastically changed.

Demographics had evolved, and South Brooklyn was now populated by Irish, Italian, and Lebanese Catholics, and by African-Americans and Latinos who belonged to fundamentalist Christian sects. As these new populations increased, the Methodist congregation withered, its minister left, and eventually the church closed its doors.

When Smith arrived on Warren Street, gone was the vibrancy of the church, but as he would soon discover, just outside its walls vigor and vitality abounded.

The parsonage where he lived was separated from the church by a narrow, dark alley that led from the street into a dirt yard that was a popular, but somewhat eerie place where neighborhood children played. The front and rear doors of the parsonage opened onto roof covered porches connected to the street by wooden steps. The porches and steps were popular hangouts for neighborhood kids, and often the sites of card games. Across the street from the front of the church stood the massive, four-story, windowless, doorless brick wall of a furniture warehouse. The wall provided neighborhood kids with an ideal surface for playing handball and homemade games named "Ivanhoe" and "Donkey". The street in front of the church was the best fist ball court in the neighborhood, and except during the winter, games were played there almost every day.

As Smith went about his custodial duties, he became acquainted with some of the neighborhood boys. When a group of them asked about the possibility of using the large, heated meeting hall in the church basement as a place to play on cold winter days, Smith saw a great opportunity.

Approaching the Board of the Methodist Church, he proposed that the vacant basement be used to develop a non-sectarian community center. The Board was supportive and some of its members donated and raised funds to equip the facility, and to convert the basement into a basketball court.

Smith spurred the formation of the United Boys Club, and later, when there was a critical number of girls coming to the Center, the United Girls Club. All club members were responsible for helping maintain the facility. This included sweeping floors, painting walls, minor carpentry, emptying trashcans, moving furniture, shoveling snow, cleaning rest rooms and a host of other chores. Each year nominations and campaigns preceded the election of club officers who had responsibility for establishing rules of conduct, and for deciding how the center would be used. The clubs held regular open meetings and eventually published their own newsletter.

After a few years a generous couple, Charles and Maude Hardie, donated about two hundred acres of land near Monroe, New York to be developed into a summer camp. It was named Camp Glen Hardie.

Everyone in the neighborhood referred to the Warren Street Community Center as "the gym." Not long after my teammates and I started going to the gym, the pastor of St. Paul's Church announced from the pulpit one Sunday morning, that parents must prohibit their children from going to the gym. He warned that the gym was sponsored by a Protestant church and that people at the gym would try to convert their children to become Methodists. He was emphatic that it was the duty of parents to enforce the ban.

When my parents told me that I was no longer to go to there, I countered there was nothing religious going on at the gym. They did not budge: If the pastor said not to go to the gym, then I was not to go there. Well, that order had about as much chance of being effective as telling an Iowa hog to watch its table manners. To the pastor and my parents, the issue might have been religion: to me, the issue was basketball.

I continued to play at the gym and eventually my parents dropped the subject. Most of my teammates were Catholic and they continued to play at the gym. At least half of the kids who went there were from Catholic families, and it was not obvious that the pastor's proclamation influenced attendance.

The basketball court, formerly a basement congregational meeting hall, was about 70% the size of a regulation court and had some odd features.

Its small size did not allow for sidelines or out-of-bounds space: if the ball hit the wall, it was out of bounds. Players hitting the wall under the basket were part of the game. Speeding to the basket, releasing the ball on the fly, twisting your body in mid-air -like an Olympic diver off the high board- you learned to angle a body roll off the wall, if you were to avoid getting creamed .

Dribbling the ball, "dead spots" were encountered, places where the ball stopped bouncing, because the floorboards were loose. At one spot, the floor bulged slightly upward causing the ball to bounce back quicker, and usually at a surprising angle.

Along the base of one of the sidewalls, a six-inch heating pipe ran the length of the court, and was another source of erratic bounces.

The court had a low ceiling: shots from a distance hit the ceiling if they had much arc. Staying aware of the score could be a problem, because there was no scoreboard

In one corner of the court, a door opened to a flight of concrete stairs leading down to the furnace room. This door was virtually always closed, but during one game, it became open. As my teammate Anthony raced down the court, his eye on the basket, he left his feet and released a beautiful, over-the-head hook shot. Airborne and expecting to roll off the wall, he rotated his body, but then disappeared into the furnace room as the ball cleanly swished through the net, scoring two points. Sore, cut, scraped and shaken, he crawled up the stairs, and sat out the rest of the game. Fortunately, he had not broken any bones or sustained any serious injuries.

Two years after our team began to play at the gym, Smith and the Board of the Methodist Church had raised funds to renovate the rest of the Church building. What had been the Church Sanctuary was converted into a full-size basketball court with high ceilings, sideline space, a scoreboard, and a floor without tricky spots. The new court even eliminated the need to roll off the wall when making a layup shot.

Chapter Nine

Smith saw talent and potential in everyone, and had a knack for making each kid feel special. There was a wide spectrum of abilities, attitudes, interests and behavior amongst the more that 100 youngsters who came to the gym. Many, but not all, were interested in playing basketball. Others just wanted a place to hang out. Some were real tough mugs, a few were sociopaths, but most were just regular kids.

The overall bedlam of the place, doors slamming as kids came and went; feet and basketballs pounding the wooden floor boards, background ruckus from the constant chatter and laughter, none of this seemed to interfere with Smith getting to know everyone who came to the gym. Leaning against the railing, he oversaw the goings on from his perch on the balcony, while engaging teenagers in conversations that ranged from sports and movies, to human rights, democratic societies, and ethical behavior.

Not everything at the gym evolved around basketball. When some boys showed an interest in crafts, he arranged for a neighborhood carpenter to come to the gym and supervise some shop classes. When a kid showed some interest in music, drawing or reading, Smith found ways to promote it. From time to time he would take a group of boys interested in music to a Saturday afternoon performance at the Metropolitan Opera. They would sit in the upper balcony, up with the aficionados, up where some people with standing room tickets played chess behind the last row, hearing but not seeing the opera.

One of Smith's favorite subjects was the responsibility of individuals in a free society. Once, after several conversations about this, he took a bunch of us to see a Broadway performance of Arthur Miller's adaptation of Ibsen's "An Enemy of the People". Most of us had never been to Broadway before; none of us had ever seen a live play with professional actors.

Smith was a man of action, who also taught by example. One evening two gangs were milling and confronting in the street in front of the gym. Hearing about it, Smith went outside, where some knives had already been displayed. He stepped into the street and loudly began lecturing them that they were standing on hallowed ground, made so by George Washington and his troops during the American Revolution. Some of the hoods must have wondered who this crazy old man was. "You can not desecrate this sacred ground, and dishonor those people who fought on this very spot for your freedom -now get the hell out of here", he shouted. I have no idea what his backup plan was for this potentially dangerous situation, but none was needed. Mumbling and grumbling, the rumblers drifted away.

When I began going to the gym, Smith had a part time assistant who supervised the place in his absence, and coached and refereed basketball games. Joe Murphy had great rapport with kids. He was from a large, poor Warren Street family. His father had died from chronic alcoholism, leaving his mother penniless, and with a hoard of children to raise. With a mop of long, shiny black curls, a five o'clock shadow, a drab outfit of second-hand clothes, and an overall disheveled appearance, Joe looked like a hippie, before there were hippies.

Until she learned more about him from me, my mother, who had seen Joe on the streets many times, thought that he was a hobo. This was not an unreasonable assumption, since downtown Brooklyn had a small skid row, whose congregants spilled over into our neighborhood. On cold winter days some could be seen standing in the street, warming themselves around a fire burning inside of an oil drum, nursing a bottle of Mission Bell wine.

Joe came from a family of prizefighters. His father had boxed, and Joe and his two brothers had also fought in the ring. By the time he returned from soldiering in World War II, Joe was an avowed socialist. Using the GI Bill, he began to take courses in social work at Long Island University, but after a while dropped out. He lived frugally with two brothers whose incomes, in part, came from collecting unemployment benefits. They would take a job for a while, and finding a way to get laid off, would become eligible for 26 weeks of unemployment benefits.

Anyone who became unemployed, but had not quit his job, was eligible to receive $20 a week for 26 weeks. This was not a bad stipend when the minimum hourly wage was 40 cents, and cigarettes were 17 cents a pack. There were always a handful of young men in the neighborhood who belonged to what was called the "26-20 Club".

To receive benefits required showing up once a week at the State Unemployment Office, standing in line most of the morning, and then pursuing employment leads from the list given to you by your caseworker. It was not difficult to look unattractive to a potential employer, thereby assuring continued unemployment and uninterrupted checks.

Joe and his brothers had various schemes aimed at producing income. They bet on horse races, but lost more than they won. They regularly went to the racetrack, and spent the time between races searching through the sea of tickets on the ground, hoping to find a winning ticket that had been mistakenly discarded. They claimed that occasionally the search was successful, but they never had a bonanza.

The betting that did work for them was a dangerous game they played during the Friday night boxing matches at Madison Square Garden. Gambling at the fights was unorthodox because bets could be placed, not only before the match started, but also while it was in progress. As the fight proceeded, the odds would change, depending on which fighter appeared to be winning the bout. Even after the fight was finished, bets were being placed until the official decision was ready to be announced.

The Murphy gimmick worked because when they placed their bets at the end of a fight, they already knew who had won the fight, knew before the official decision had been announced. Their balcony seats, one at each end of Madison Square Garden, placed a Murphy behind and above each of the two official judges who scored the fight. Using binoculars and their keen knowledge of boxing, they could determine how both judges scored each round as the fight progressed.

The third official scoring the fight was the referee. Regardless of where he stood when marking his card at the end of each round, one of the Murphy brothers could see his card. The binoculars did not allow them to actually read the print on the officials' cards, but did allow them to see in which of the two columns on the card the mark was made. It was pretty straightforward to deduce which column belonged to which fighter.

With subtle hand signals and binoculars, they communicated their findings to each other, and then placed bets. Their fraudulent scheme was successful, but they used it sparingly to avoid raising suspicions. When the declared winner of a bout was not the fighter that spectators thought had won, the Murphy brothers could make a big killing.

I was always nervous when I was there with them and they were playing this dangerous game. It was obvious that some of the spectators they were bilking included some pretty tough characters. I had visions of a Murphy being launched from the balcony destined for the seats on the main floor.

Some days when Joe was not working in the gym, my buddies and I would go to his apartment to drink coffee, play cards, and as Smith would say: "Sling the bullshit". The place was always a terrible mess. In the middle of what could be considered their living room, amidst newspapers, magazines, and paper coffee cups strewn about on the floor, there was a large corrugated metal basin containing wet newspapers. Assuming the basin was for trash, one of us pitched an end stage wad of chewing gum into the basin, only to be told that it was not for trash—it was the refrigerator. Lifting the soaked papers revealed a block of ice upon which sat strips of bacon, slices of salami, and assorted items of food.

Living on a tight budget, the brothers spent the minimum on amenities. I remember that once my friend Eddie had to use the bathroom and when he was finished, could not find toilet paper. When from behind the toilet door he called out his dilemma, Joe got up, walked across the room, pushed open the door, and tossed Eddie a copy of Ring Magazine that had been lying on the floor.

We saw a lot of Joe: he coached our basketball team, and in the summer he worked with Smith at the Community Center's summer camp near Monroe, New York. For kids from Brooklyn, Camp Glen Hardie was like heaven: campfires with stories and roasted marshmallows every night; swimming every day; horseback riding; softball games; fishing; and overnight hikes to explore an abandoned iron ore mine. Excursions to historic spots in the Hudson River Valley, a day at the local county fair, a visit to the Baseball Hall of Fame at Cooperstown, New York, a trip to George Washington's Headquarters at Newburgh, New York -all of this, and two weeks of great meals prepared by Henry Clay Smith -for the grand total of five dollars. If your family could not afford to pay, you went to camp for free.

Through a friend, Smith met Mrs. Hertz, who donated two station wagons to the camp. Loaded with kids, and with Smith driving one, and Joe Murphy the other, the caravan made the round trip between Warren Street and Monroe every two weeks, bright yellow Hertz Corporation logos conspicuously on display. Depending on what was ready to be picked in Smith's garden, the campers returned to Brooklyn with corn, tomatoes, cucumbers and peppers for their families.

All campers had daily chores: washing dishes, setting tables, cleaning cabins and tents, policing grounds, gathering and chopping firewood, weeding the vegetable garden, picking tomatoes and corn, and everyone's favorite—cleaning the outhouse.

The camp accommodated 10 to 12 kids per group, and exemplified ethnic and racial diversity before that term was coined. Four boys and a counselor slept in one of the two small wooden cabins, or in an Army surplus tent. Smith's quarters were on a farm across the highway from the camp. He could never have gotten a decent night's sleep had he not arranged to stay at the farm.

Campers were awakened each day about 6:00 a.m. by the sounds of Smith singing "O What a Beautiful Morning" as he walked across the campgrounds on his way to cook breakfast. The camp kitchen was an open porch on the back of one of the cabins. It was equipped with two Coleman stoves. There was no refrigerator, because there was no electricity at the camp. Campers hauled water from a hand-pumped well.

Camp was a fun two weeks in the country, but its most meaningful aspect was the contact with Smith, an experience that would not immediately be appreciated, but whose influence would grow with time. Coming from a Catholic background, where guilt and fear were the forces that attempted to modify inherent behavior, it was a new experience to be around a person who seemed to be guided by humane, egalitarian principles, not assigned or enforced from without, but determined from within.

Chapter Ten

When I was 14, second in priority to basketball was generating pocket money. This was accomplished piecemeal by numerous means.

One way was to do day jobs for a Syrian man in the neighborhood who made his living with his truck. When he had a job moving a household, and it was not a school day, he would pay each of us five dollars to do the grunt work of loading and unloading the truck.

Another way to generate income was to set pins in a bowling alley. There were several bowling alleys in downtown Brooklyn where pinsetters were hired on a day-to-day basis. You showed up late in the afternoon and if they needed someone, you had a job for that evening. Most of the people who set pins were drifters or men from skid row. There was no paperwork involved. The owner didn't know your name, and didn't need to.

Setting pins was a noisy, potentially hazardous way to earn a few dollars. A pinsetter worked out of sight in a pit at the end of the alley. The work paid ten cents per bowler, per game. If a party of four was bowling, then you earned forty cents per game. In order to make it worth your while, it was necessary to simultaneously set the pins on two adjacent lanes.

When the bowling ball struck the pins, both the ball and pins came flying into the pit.

Like Jack in the rhyme, you had to be nimble and quick. Nimble to avoid being hit by the ball or the pins: quick to keep the customers and the boss happy. After the collision of ball and pins, the setter dropped into the pit from his perch above, grabbed the ball, sent it back to the bowler, stepped on a foot peddle that elevated ten metallic pegs from the floor, and placed a bowling pin on each peg. You quickly learned to handle two pins at a time with each hand.

The emphasis was on speed. For the boss, time was money: the shorter the game, the more games that got played. For the bowlers, when they picked up a ball, they wanted to bowl, not wait for pins to be set. For the guy in the pit, the happier the boss, the more likely you would work there again; the happier the bowlers, the more likely you would get a good tip.

Baaba, G-man, The Gee, Honey, Burpy, Chizzy, Bubsy, Skeets, Zorro, Yummie, Popeye, Bula, Tiny, Frenchy, Nuke, Bingo, Jocko – the neighborhood was full of kids with nicknames.

One of my best friends was a Puerto Rican boy named Angelo. Everyone, including his mother, father, brothers and sisters had always called him Spicky. This never seemed to bother him, until he reached 17. Then he let everyone know that he wanted to be called Angelo. From then on, out on the street, he was Angelo. But even a year later, when his mother answered my knock at their door and I asked if Angelo was home, she told me: "No, Spicky's not here".

Angelo was a master at what was called "junking". Junking involved stripping abandoned buildings of lead pipes, copper rain gutters, and anything else that a Third Avenue junk yard would pay cash for.

Once I went junking with Angelo in some dilapidated buildings near the Brooklyn Bridge. Formerly housing, the buildings had been condemned by the City and were scheduled for demolition. Officially, these buildings were unoccupied, but after all the families had moved out, winos, drifters and other homeless persons began to squat in them.

After a couple of hours of hacking out lead pipes and disconnecting rain downspouts, we compacted the metal, loaded our gunny sacks, flipped them over our shoulders, and headed for the junk yards. While hurrying along Fulton Street -one of the busiest streets in downtown Brooklyn—I spied my Aunt Margaret on the other side of the crowded street. I was pretty sure she hadn't seen me, but if she had, I knew she would want to know: "What's in the sack?"

Reaching Third Avenue we found a place that was buying scrap metal. The junk yards payed for cooper and lead by the pound. Angelo and I split about ten dollars, which was a lot of money to a teenager.

When I reached home that evening, the first words out of my mother's mouth were: "Your Aunt Margaret saw you running down Fulton Street this afternoon".

At this point, I was sure it was curtains.

"She said you looked filthy and had a hole in the back of your pants".

I waited for more, but it never came: not a word about the sack. I was saved by my Aunt's fixation on dress.

I had an abortive start at going into business for myself, but it was vehemently squashed by my parents. Seeing that other kids, including my friends Angelo and Leo, earned money shining shoes on the streets, I built a shoeshine box intending to work the busy streets around Borough Hall in downtown Brooklyn.

After building the box, I proudly showed it to my parents. Revealing my plan proved to be a tactical error: they were adamant that I would not be a shoeshine boy. I was amazed at their response and its basis: it was a matter of family pride with a racial nuance.

They believed that the kids who shined shoes -most of them were black or Hispanic- had to do it because their families were poor. Having a shoeshine boy in the family would have been an embarrassment to my mother and father. "What would the neighbors think"?

Angelo once asked me to sleep over because his father needed some help moving furniture. They lived in a three-room apartment, in the front half of the top floor of a four story tenement building on Wyckoff Street. The parents slept in one room, the four boys and two girls slept in the largest room, a drape separating the boys and girls. By day it was the living room, at night it became the bedroom. The third room was a small kitchen.

In the middle of the night Angelo's father woke us, and said it was time to move a couch. It seemed like a strange time to be moving furniture. Angelo told me that a new couch had been purchased, and was to be delivered later that day. The delivery men would not remove the old couch, without being paid extra. This was understandable considering the narrow hallways and steep stairs between the street and the fourth floor. Nonetheless, the old couch had to go to make room for the new one, and Angelo's father was not going to pay some extra charge.

Leaving all lights unlit, Angelo's father took a screwdriver and began removing the child safety barrier from one of the windows. When this was done, he instructed Manny, one of Angelo's younger brothers, to go down to the street and make sure there were not any people around. When Manny gave the all clear signal from down below, Angelo, his father and I lifted the couch, slid it along the window sill, and on a whispered count of three—pushed it out of the window. It made one hell of a noise when it hit the street. Manny quickly returned, the window was closed, and we all went back to bed.

The best paying job I had as a teenager was delivering groceries on Saturdays for a delicatessen on Montague Street, in the Brooklyn Heights. The pay was forty cents an hour, but most people tipped quite generously. My brother Jim worked afternoons and Saturdays at the deli and helped me get the job.

Brooklyn Heights was a residential area populated by wealthy people, artists, writers, and a host of celebrities. One of the customers I delivered groceries to was the playwright Arthur Miller. Another was Eugene Dennis, Secretary General of the American Communist Party. Across the street from the delicatessen was the Bossert Hotel. Burt Shotton, the manager of the Brooklyn Dodgers, and some of the baseball team's players roomed at the Bossert and sometimes shopped at the deli. After a couple of years the deli changed ownership, and my job was eliminated.

One summer I started a job in a printing company near the Brooklyn Navy Yard. I didn't last very long. The company was located on the top floor of a large warehouse building where several enormous printing presses that produced large glossy sheets that contained the uncut pages of books. As the sheets came off the presses, they moved onto large wooden skids. When a skid was full, it was my job to move it to the truck-loading platform on the street level. I accomplished this using a hand-pulled forklift and the building's freight elevator.

The concrete floor of the plant was full of chuckholes. If you moved the loaded forklift too slowly, it was apt to have a wheel get stuck in a chuckhole. When this happened, it required a lot of pushing, pulling, rocking and muscle to get the forklift moving again. In order to assure not getting the forklift stuck halfway onto the elevator—a situation that created a terrible problem—it was necessary to move the loaded forklift aboard with a bit of momentum, but then stop before crashing into the far wall of the elevator shaft. Each time the weight of the load hit the elevator's floor, the car sank several inches and I flinched, wondering if this was the load that would break the elevator cable and send everything—including me—on an express trip to the bottom of the shaft.

While every employee had specific jobs, all of us had a common job: we were firemen. Several times each day a sheet coming off a press would get stuck over the row of open flame jets that dried the ink before the sheet fell onto the skid. When the alarm sounded everyone dropped what they were doing and tackled the fire. Working on a floor crowded with mounds of paper and flammable liquids, every employee took fires seriously, recognizing that time did not permit waiting for the NYFD.

After I had worked there for a few days, I noticed that on a wall in the men's rest room, written in chalk, in very large print, there were a series of numbers. After a while I realized that the numbers were different each day. Not giving it much thought, I assumed the numbers had something to do with the union-organizing activities that were going on. When I mentioned the numbers to my foreman, I learned that it was the winning lottery number of the previous day, and that a bookie's runner, who came each day to collect bets from the employees, wrote the numbers on the wall. Presumably, the numbers were also posted in the women's rest room, since they were some of the most avid gamblers.

After about two months I quit the job because it was pure grunt work. I wasn't learning much, my hands were taking a beating from the printed sheets whose edges were like razor blades, and I saw no future for me in the printing business. As I was leaving on my last day, I controlled a wise-ass impulse to advise the foreman that he consider replacing me with a mule.

The spring that I turned 16, several friends and I began leaving NYC on weekends. Usually it was to go with Smith to Monroe, to help him get Camp Glen Hardie ready for the summer. These were weekends full of work; preparing the ground, planting the vegetable garden, hauling gravel to repair the campground roads, clearing, chopping and burning fallen tree limbs, painting furniture and the camp rowboat, grooming the hiking trails, and positioning the outhouses over the new pits we had dug. All this manual labor by growing teenagers results in big appetites.

Talented in the kitchen, Smith always put out a hefty spread. Many evenings the dinner conversations ranged from history to baseball, to educational psychology, to secularism and religion. Being around Smith was a new kind of educational experience. Sometimes he would mention a person none of us had ever heard of before and this would lead to learning something about the ideas of thinkers like the psychoanalyst Eric Fromm, the philosopher John Dewey, and the theologian Rabbi Joshua Lieberman. I never got the impression that Smith was promoting any particular viewpoint but rather, he was challenging us to become informed and to think.

Used to seeing us leave for on a weekend, our parents assumed that when we were gone, we were at Smith's camp. Sometimes we were; sometimes we weren't.

Four of us had developed strong wanderlust and began hitchhiking on some weekends with the idea of seeing new places. We made trips to Montreal, Boston, the Adirondack Mountains, Lake George and Washington, DC. We usually slept in a field, a park, the back seat of a moving car, or a big city train or bus station. We traveled in pairs, agreeing in advance to meet at a designated place. Sometimes this worked, other times we never saw the other pair until we were back in Brooklyn.

We had some interesting experiences. On a trip to Washington, DC, my friend Emilio and I were standing in a pouring rain on a New Jersey roadside, our thumbs out, when a car passed, pulled onto the shoulder, and stopped. Happy to get out of the rain, we ran to the car and got into the back seat. Once the car started moving, it was immediately obvious that the car did not have a windshield.

The ride was hair-raising because the driver, who was wearing goggles, was a bit of a nut case. The rain and the force of the air rushing into the car made it difficult to see the road, and we were getting soaked. We drove for over an hour, but when he reached his turnoff point, we were glad to get out of the car.

Later that evening, moments after getting a ride outside of Laurel, Maryland, a state police car, lights flashing, came along side, and signaled our driver to pull off the road. The trooper had obviously seen the driver stop and pick us up, because he immediately lectured him about the law against picking up hitchhikers. The trooper had us get into the back seat of his vehicle, and began asking questions. We gave our names, told him we were from Brooklyn, and that we were headed for Washington, where we were to meet our two buddies at the train station.

He drove us to the State Police barracks, where we were interrogated by another officer. When the questioning was finished, we were taken downstairs. As we entered the basement there was commotion and swearing coming from the end of the corridor where there were two adjacent cells. One was empty, the other was crowded with African-American men, some sober, some not. Ignoring their questions and complaints, the trooper unlocked the empty cell, told us to get in, and then locked the door behind us.

The cells were probably designed for single occupancy. On the floor outside of the cell was a bucket. The trooper told us that if we had to take a leak, "aim through the bars and get it all in the bucket". Then he left. Some of our neighbors wanted to know what we had done, but most of them were just bitching while involved in loud four-way conversations.

Emilio and I were worried because it was not clear what was going to happen. We spent all night in the cell, but it was impossible to sleep. There was a single bench without a pad, the lights were always on, and there was constant talking, complaining and commotion as people were taken from the adjacent cell to appear before a judge, and new arrivals replaced them.

Early Saturday morning a tray of food appeared and then a trooper came and took Emilio away. I didn't see him again until I was back in Brooklyn. About midday, another trooper unlocked the cell, took me upstairs, and told me I was being released. I was given some money that had been wired from New York by my mother, and was told to buy a bus ticket and return home.

At the bus station I was still worried that my two friends would be waiting at the DC train station, so I decided to buy a ticket to Washington. After searching the train station and not finding them, I bought a bus ticket and returned to New York.

When I arrived home, it was Sunday morning and my mother was sitting in the living room with my Uncle Eddie, who was a New York City policeman. Not knowing what was next, I sat and listened. I learned that when the Maryland State Police called, my parents were beside themselves. They had no idea what was going on, least of all, what I was doing in Maryland. My mother immediately phoned her brother Ed, asking for help.

I learned from my uncle that on the evening Emilio and I left Brooklyn, a boy had been killed in a gang fight in South Brooklyn. Police departments along the East Coast were alerted and informed that the unknown assailants were still on the loose. When the state trooper learned that Emilio and I were from Brooklyn, and had left there on Friday evening, he made the connection.

Considering what had to be a weekend of stress and worry for them, I found my parent's reaction to these unannounced travels rather benign. Possibly they wondered whether naming me after my Uncle Richie had been such a good idea..

On another Friday evening, my friend Paddy and I headed for the Adirondacks, intending to make it to the top of Whiteface Mountain.

We got stranded about 1:00 a.m. on the outskirts of Poughkeepsie, New York. Experience told us that accepting a ride at this late hour increased the risk of having to deal with a drunken driver or worse: we decided to walk further and find a place to sleep. We soon came upon a stand of tall evergreens with long dense branches and soft beds of dried needles beneath them, an ideal shelter, so we bedded down for the night.

The sounds of voices nearby awakened us to a chilly, damp morning. Through the early morning fog, a scene appeared that was surreal: pairs of adults—some men, some women, some in street clothes, some in robes—engaged in conversations, and slowly promenading, arm in arm, across a large, neatly manicured lawn. What had appeared in the dark the night before to be the edge of a forest, turned out early in the morning to be the grounds of a state mental hospital. Without fanfare, we were gone.

From time to time Smith allowed a few of us to spend a weekend at the camp without him. We stayed in a small cabin on the property, and performed some maintenance work there. We also spent some time hunting. In retrospect, some of our actions elevated the practice of stupidity to levels rarely achieved.

Jocko, an older boy with access to a car, usually was part of the weekend group. This made getting to Monroe a simple matter. On a few occasions when he did not go, those who did would hitchhike. I recall one weekend when Emilio and I, with dissembled shotguns wrapped inside of blankets underarm, rode the subway from Brooklyn to the George Washington Bridge, hopped a bus to Fort Lee, New Jersey, and thumbed rides to Monroe.

The cabin at the camp was not insulated, but did have a pot-bellied coal stove. Because the heat from the stove rose to the top of the house, on cold Fall nights we would remove the closet and bedroom doors from their hinges, lay them across the ceiling joists, toss our sleeping bags up, and sleep where the heat accumulated. That is, everyone except Emilio who, although he was very strong, was unable to chin himself up between the joists and onto our ad hoc loft.

One particularly cold night, after the lights had been turned out, and three of us were up above starting to get to sleep, Emilio was down below, bitching about the cold, messing with the stove, and trying to get more heat out of it. All at once, there was an explosion, accompanied by a blinding light, as if the sun had risen inside of the cabin.

Had we rehearsed it, the three of us above could not have descended with greater synchrony, suave, or speed. Landing on our feet with the grace of trained gymnasts, we found the door of the pot-bellied stove wide open, bright flames reaching out, and Emilio, moaning and groaning, laying on the floor at the opposite end of the room. Never particularly savvy or patient, when adding more coal failed to provide the heat he wanted, Emilio had opened the top of the stove and poured in a cup of Coleman fuel. The explosion blew him clear across the room.

After lifting him onto a couch and covering him with blankets, someone suggested that rubbing butter onto his burned arms would provide some soothing relief. This being accomplished, three of us returned to the loft, crawled into our sleeping bags and, to the sounds of staccato whimpering from the darkness below, fell asleep.

It bordered on insanity that teenagers from Brooklyn were walking around the woods of Orange County, New York with loaded shotguns. None of us had been trained in firearm safety, but in New York State that was not mandatory. As long as we had valid hunting licenses, nothing we were doing was illegal.

One of my scariest moments happened while walking with Emilio on a hilly gravel road alongside a lake, each with a shotgun in hand, hoping to find some ducks. The morning was cool enough to be wearing my khaki Army surplus parka, but not cool enough to have its fur-lined hood pulled over my head. Emilio was walking behind me. All at once there was quacking overhead. Reflexively, Emilio jerked his shotgun up to shoot. I felt my hood being yanked. I froze, instantly knowing what had happened. The end of his shotgun barrel was snagged in the hood of my parka and he was trying to tug it free. I would not be here writing this, had he pulled the trigger.

We had a rule that a gun would never be taken into the cabin, until it had been rendered incapable of firing. For a shotgun that was easy: the barrel was removed. For a bolt-action rifle, the bolt, which contains the firing pin- was removed. For some rifles, it was more complicated. One of my friends, Charley-boy, owned a lever-action 30/30 rifle. Because it was not a simple matter to dissemble that rifle for safety purposes, the rule was it could never be in the house if it was loaded.

One evening, while Charley-boy was sitting on the couch oiling the barrel and wooden stock of his 30/30 and the rest of us were playing cards, someone looked up, noticed the rifle, and asked if it was loaded. With great confidence, Charley-boy replied that it was not loaded. As a reassuring afterthought, he pointed the rifle upward, pulled the trigger and bam!, blasted a hole in the roof of the cabin. He couldn't believe it; we couldn't believe it. Repairing the roof was easy; thinking about what could had happened was terrifying.

Even now, recalling those near-misses triggers an eerie visceral sensation that radiates internally from my groin, the same kind of gonadal reflex I've had when standing on the rim and looking directly down into the Grand Canyon, or when leaning against a glass panel at the top of the Sears Tower and looking straight down to the streets below.

The stupidity we displayed handling firearms during our short careers as hunters from the big city, while ridiculous, was outdone by another big city hunter whose escapade I read about on the front page of a New York City newspaper when I was a teenager. Returning from a seemingly successful hunting trip in upstate New York, his trophy proudly on display for all to see, the man was stopped for speeding by a New Jersey State Trooper. While writing the summons, the trooper asked why there was a domestic goat strapped across one of the car's fenders. At least Emilio and I knew Mallards from barnyard ducks.

For Smith's peace of mind, he went to his grave never knowing about these events.

Chapter Eleven

After leaving high school in June, 1952, I spent the summer working for Smith at Camp Glen Hardie. The job was a mix of helping with the campers, and being an unskilled laborer. By summer's end, I had become a semi-skilled laborer.

One of Smith's dreams for the camp was a building that would house the camp kitchen and dining hall, a community room for rainy day activities, quarters for some staff, a garage, a maintenance shop, and a washroom with toilets and plumbing for the campers.

Funds were not available to have a contractor do the job, so Smith decided he would learn how to build the facility. He read and took notes from how-to-do-it books on foundations, masonry, carpentry and roofing. He generated lists of questions and then tapped the heads of knowledgeable persons for answers. When he saw a house under construction, he would stop, look and ask questions.

With the help of relatives, friends and alumni who had engineering and architectural experience, a set of blue prints was created. When the spring thaw arrived in 1952, wooden stakes outlining the building's foundation were pounded into the ground, and trenches five feet deep were dug. It was all pick axes, sledge hammers, shovels, wheel barrels and muscle: not a piece of heavy equipment was involved.

When it came time to pour the concrete foundation, we used an old panel truck to haul gravel from a local hillside, sand from an open pit, water from the camp's hand-pumped well and bags of cement from a local supplier. The concrete components were placed in a large metal pan and mixed by hand with hoes. When the appropriate consistency of the mix was reached, the concrete was shoveled into a wheelbarrow and poured into the trenches. Iron rods, bars and other pieces of scrap metal previously collected by Smith were pushed into the poured concrete to reinforce it and to provide connectors to the cinder blocks that would form the walls of the first level of the building.

Sections of the wooden frame of the building were constructed from two by fours, cut with handsaws and then nailed together. When it came time to set the rafters, it was a day of ropes, pulleys and muscle. Teaching as he worked, Smith showed how to have the tools, rather than our arms, do most of the work, and expounded on why joints had to be made with pieces of lumber that had been cut perfectly square. Quickly we became skilled at making square cuts and sinking nails accurately. Throughout the building's construction, the standards for structural integrity were routinely exceeded, prompting a visiting engineer to once ask Smith if he was building a hurricane shelter.

Besides Smith and a handful of teenage boys, the work was done by alumni of the Warren Street Community Center who volunteered on weekends and during their summer vacations. Some came because they had pleasant memories from their days at Camp Glen Hardie, others came because Smith had been such a positive influence on their lives. A few came because, had it not been for Smith, they might be doing time in a clink: everyone came because it was a chance to do something for Smith.

One who came was my good friend, Johnny-boy. He was from a poor and dysfunctional Irish family. When he was born all of his sibs were already young adults. His mother and alcoholic father had died before he was ten. Raised by his sister in a small, cold water flat where two brothers, both severe alcoholics prone to violent behavior also lived, Johnny-boy's home life was bleak.

He was a street-wise and physical kid who had learned early on to fend for himself. His usual garb was Army-Navy store surplus or charity shop hand-me-downs. A missing incisor and scars on his forehead and chin were advertisements of a life that had already logged lots of miles. In spite of his tough mug appearance, if you spent much time around Johnny-boy, you had to like him. Fundamentally a decent person, loyal to friends, never a bully or a coward, he was by nature suspicious, and if threatened could become violent, even dangerous.

At school his progress was slow and with time he became older and bigger than his classmates. During his last year at St. Paul's the nuns removed him from class and assigned him to work with the school janitor. He never attended high school, and while he came to the gym, he was not interested in or adept at sports. When he was about 16, he began to hang out with a gang of bad apples. It was not long until he and some of his new associates were arrested for a burglary.

When Johnny-boy's case was heard in Juvenile Court, Smith attended with the intention of informing the judge about the miserable conditions in which Johnny-boy was raised, and stating his believe that a jail sentence could destroy any chance at rehabilitation. He wanted to request a sentence of probation and was prepared to take personal responsibility for Johnny-boy, and to give him a job. At the hearing, the judge was not receptive to Smith injecting himself into the proceedings. When he persisted, the judge threatened to hold him in contempt of court. Smith was not to be muzzled. Activating a sparingly used flare for the dramatic, he told the judge that having already lived most of his life, he was not worried about the consequences of being held in contempt of court—his concern was for giving this kid the chance he never had to become a useful member of society. He added that if held in contempt he was entitled to a phone call, and he would be making it to his brother-in-law, who was a law partner of Thomas Dewey, the Governor of New York.

Amazingly, the judge allowed Smith to speak, and at the end of the hearing assigned probation. Smith hired Johnny-boy to work at the Community Center. While there were a few alcohol-related bumps in the road along the way, through his work with Smith, Johnny-boy became drawn to life in the country. He eventually married, and not wanting to raise children in a big city, moved to a small town in the Adirondacks, where he raised a family, and worked in a lumber mill until he died in his sixties.

As the end of summer approached, the big question for me was: What's next"?

I had a long list of things I knew I didn't want to do, but a list of negatives didn't answer the question. My father wanted me to return home and find a job. I knew I would be getting my draft notice in a few months, so taking a job for a short time was not appealing. My father's idea of a good job was white collar office work in an insurance company, white collar for status and insurance company for security—"they didn't layoff workers during the Depression". But after a summer in the country, working outdoors, wearing boots, Levi's and a t-shirt, the idea of a shirt and tie job in New York City sounded awful.

At the beginning of August, my best friend, Paddy Finnerty, arrived at camp to help with the construction work. He had spent the summer taking college classes, and had received notice from his draft board to report for duty in the Army in October.

Both soon to be property of Uncle Sam, we decided to spend September exploring New York State, getting from place to place by hitchhiking, and supporting ourselves with odd jobs. On Smith's recommendation a farmer hired us as day laborers at a large apple orchard near New Paltz, New York. Migrant agricultural workers, all African American families from the South, had already begun the harvest. Wary of the damage that could be inflicted by two inexperienced workers leaning ladders against his apple trees, the farmer hired us to pick "drops", apples on the ground under the trees.

We earned 10 cents for each bushel basket filled. The work was tough on the hands and knees. It required scurrying about on all fours, grabbing apples with both hands, tossing them into the basket we dragged along, all the while trying to avoid kneeling on an apple. The dew on the grass assured that after starting each morning, your pants and feet would soon be soaked. Beneath the trees the ground cover contained poison ivy vines, and the air buzzed with bees interested in the same bruised and softening apples you hoped to put into your basket. Once filled, you lugged the basket to a nearby wagon, exchanging it for a paper chit that could later be exchanged for cash.

The migrant workers were quartered in paltry facilities on the orchard grounds. We had hoped to sleep at the orchard, but the farmer was adamant that he would not allow two white boys to spend nights there. Paddy and I rented a room in a boarding house in New Paltz, and while it was a nice place, it was an unplanned expense.

To compensate, each evening we hitchhiked the 7 miles back and forth between New Paltz and Poughkeepsie, where we set pins in a bowling alley. After about two weeks, the apple harvest was complete. We had saved enough money, so instead of moving on with the migrant workers who had invited us to join them to pick another crop, we decided to travel and sightsee.

At the end of September, Paddy and I returned to Brooklyn. He was getting ready to report for his induction physical at 39 Whitehall Street in Manhattan, an address well known to young men in the

New York area; it was where you were inducted regardless of what service you were entering. In "Alice's Restaurant", Arlo Guthrie Jr. had some very funny lines describing his experiences there.

My father was turning the heat up about my getting a job. When his patience had become exhausted, he issued an ultimatum: "Get a job, or move out! You have until the first of November".

In retrospect, his pronouncement was one of the best things that ever happened to me.

I decided to enlist instead of waiting to be drafted. And the sooner the better. My game plan was to sign up for the service that would take me soonest, Air Force, Navy or Marines. The Air Force and Navy were appealing because they offered the best chances to learn a trade and see the world. Given the choice of being a foot soldier in the Army or in the Marines, the latter outfit was preferable because it had more pizazz.

The Navy was able to take me soonest, so I went to their office at the Brooklyn Post Office Building to sign the papers.

Sitting at his desk, the paperwork spread out before him, the Navy recruiter asked: "How long do you want to enlist for?"

I replied: "What are the choices"?

"You can sign up for four years or six years".

Being a real dope, I said, "Put me down for six".

Glancing up with a look somewhere between surprise and disbelief, he countered: "Why don't you try it for four? Then, if you like it, you can sign up for more."

I enlisted for four years. Over time I came to realize that I owed that recruiter a tremendous debt. He could have improved his numbers by signing me up for six years. I've always been sorry that I never met him again; if I had, I would have kissed him.

I was never sure how my father felt about this outcome; he already had a son, my brother Jim, who was in a Marine combat unit in Korea. I had the sense that he was relieved: a course had been charted, I was no longer just spinning my wheels.

When the big morning arrived, I hugged my parents and family goodbye, and made the trip to 39 Whitehall. After passing my physical, raising my hand, and repeating the oath, a salty Navy Chief marched a group of us down Chambers Street to the Hudson River, where we rode the Erie Ferry to Hoboken, boarded a train, and headed for Chicago and the Great Lakes Naval Training Center.

After a fine meal in the dining car—the tab picked up by the U.S. Government—I remember climbing a ladder into a warm Pullman berth and laying there thinking: "This isn't half bad".

I dozed off, but later was awakened by the Doppler shifting sounds of warning alarms and flashing red lights as the train sped through railroad crossings.

It was after midnight when the train slowed to pass through a station. Out the window I saw signs that read: Elmira, New York. The only thing I knew about Elmira was it had a prison. I had learned that from Nick, a Court Street barber who periodically closed his shop for the day to visit a relative, who was a prisoner at Elmira.

As the train passed through the station, I had no idea that sound asleep in a house a short walk from the station, there was a beautiful eleven year old girl with long blond curls. That I would learn ten years later, when we would meet, fall in love, and spend the rest of our lives together.

Chapter Twelve

The pleasant, upscale accommodations on the train created a misleading introduction to Navy life.

One of my first encounters upon arriving at Boot Camp was with a Navy barber. Without waiting for a reply after asking how I preferred my hair to be cut, he made a series of rapid swipes at my head with his electric shears. In about a minute he was finished, and I stepped from his chair, with ears bigger and lower, and a head resembling a bowling ball.

After removing our civilian clothes, destined for shipment back home, we stood barefoot, bald and naked inside of a large, warehouse. Each of us was issued a white cotton sac with ties on one end to be used as a mattress cover. We were told to tie it around our neck and hold it open as we made our way along a counter running the length of the warehouse. Standing behind the counter at intervals were naval storekeepers, who, as you passed by, tossed into the mattress cover prescribed numbers of shirts, hats, shoes, socks, underwear, and all the other items of clothing the Navy issued to incoming enlisted men. If you were unsure of your size, the storekeeper looked you over, made a guess, and using your chest as a backboard, bank-shot the item into your mattress cover. After the Navy barber most of us were wrong about our hat size.

At the end of the counter stood a Navy Medic who with the accuracy of a skilled dart thrower, tossed a syringe at my shoulder, scoring a bulls eye in my deltoid muscle.

The next twelve weeks was non-stop marching, running, washing, scrubbing, saluting, shooting and calisthenics, with a couple of hair cuts and immunization boosters added on. In between we had classes on marlinspike seamanship, gunnery, small arms, firefighting, safety, survival, rules of conduct and military justice. Rumor had it that the odd taste in the food we ate was a chemical added by the Navy to neutralize libidos and raging hormones.

My drill instructor was a tough, leathery boson's mate from rural Arkansas, all business and obsessed with precision drills, long marches on the run, and fastidious neatness. Shortcomings on anyone's part triggered for the entire company more drills, marches, and middle of the night exercises termed "GI Parties". These involved scrubbing walls and polishing floors, and shoveling snow from enormous drill fields not used since the end of World War II.

In a deep gravely voice he spewed colorful comments and advice. When speaking to the company he used two terms, depending on how things were going that day. On good days we were "You people", on other days we were: "You fuckers". A favorite advisory was: "Give your soul to the Lord, because your ass is mine".

The psychological stresses and manipulations of boot camp were designed to totally subtract from each recruit all previous ties and allegiances, and to replace them with unfaltering, gung-ho dedication to military order, assigned responsibilities, and loyalty to shipmates. For the most part, it worked.

Placement tests determined where each of us would go after the basic training of boot camp. Another train ride at government expense took about 100 of us to the Naval Air Station at Norman, Oklahoma. After three months of aviation training, another set of placement exams produced some choices, and I choose the Naval Meteorology School at Lakehurst, New Jersey, because it was close New York. After four months learning about the science of weather, a list of available assignments was posted. Class rank determined when you got to pick from the list. I got to pick pretty early and Alaska sounded like an adventure, so I choose Kodiak Island.

Kodiak's remote location and small size tended to ease some of the formalities of military life. I belonged to the Meteorology Unit and worked rotating shifts in the control tower at the airfield. One officer and five enlisted men worked each eight hour shift gathering and analyzing weather reports received from ships and aircraft operating north of the Equator in the Pacific Ocean, and from ground stations in Asia and North America.

Hourly we made extensive measurements of meteorologic conditions at Kodiak. Every six hours we launched a large helium-filled balloon to which were attached instruments and a radio that transmitted data back about conditions aloft until the balloon eventually burst somewhere above 60,000 feet. Every six hours we produced and transmitted a detailed weather forecast for the Northern Pacific Ocean and the Arctic region. It was interesting and exciting work. The weather crew was safe and comfortable compared to those on the base who had assignments on aircraft or ships that operated in remote areas under some of the world's worst weather conditions.

Winter storms in the Northern Pacific Ocean are typically horrendous. They begin as minor atmospheric disturbances in the South China Sea. They rapidly intensify, driven by masses of cold dry air from Siberia and warm, moist air from the tropics. The two air masses chase each other in a counterclockwise rotation around a center of low pressure. In meteorologic terms, the system is a cyclone. Moving across the ocean without encountering topologic barriers, the system gains speed and ferocity as it goes. When it reaches the Gulf of Alaska, where Kodiak Island is located, the storm can have winds that reach 100 miles per hour and seas that have waves more that 45 feet high.

From October to March, Kodiak is pounded by one storm after another. Travel between the barracks and the airfield control tower in a jeep or station wagon was at times an adventure. The high winds, heavy snow and low temperatures, combined with the prolonged darkness of Alaskan winters, promoted indoor activities. There were lots of basketball and poker games and evenings spent drinking beer at the enlisted men's club.

Most of us owned short wave radios and went to sleep listening to great jazz and classical music on the North American Broadcast of Radio Moscow, fascinated by the biased political news reports interspersed amongst the music.

The unusual atmospheric conditions of the Far North, coupled with the effects of Northern Lights and the Magnetic North Pole resulted in sporadic reception of unexpected radio signals. Commonly heard were taxicab dispatchers in Los Angeles and small stations in rural America, where between songs by Hank Williams and Webb Pierce, radio preachers ranted and raved fire and brimstone.

Kodiak had a raw natural beauty and spectacular scenery. The extreme seasonal variation in solar light created stunning visual effects on the snow-covered mountains and the fragmented cloud layers that passed over on the backside of passing storms.

The Naval Station at Kodiak had a beautiful large ski area, and fortunately for us the Meteorology Group included a former member of the University of Colorado Ski Team who loved to teach.. He made it easy for a beginner to ski, and the absence of trees on most of Kodiak forgave slow learners.

After Kodiak I was assigned to a Naval Air Station at Seattle, Washington which was fabulous duty because the station was officially closed and a skeleton crew was there only in case a military aircraft in the Pacific Northwest needed an emergency landing strip. Our job was to produce weather forecasts for the military bases in the Pacific Northwest and for U.S. Navy ships operating in the offshore waters.

Five months later I was assigned to an LST, a shallow draft ship with a crew of 70 headed for the Arctic Ocean as part of a Task Force to construct a Defense Early Warning System (DEW Line) across the top of Alaska and Canada. Engaged in an escalating confrontation with the Soviet Union, the U.S. constructed radar stations in the far north to detect Soviet intercontinental missiles coming to the United States via a polar route.

Some days our voyage across the Northern Pacific Ocean in the flat-bottomed LST was like riding the Cyclone at Coney Island. Since LST's have a draft of only seven feet and do not have a keel, in stormy conditions they heel from side to side, sometimes listing more than 40 degrees in enormous waves. The noise and vibrations created as the ship's bow plowed into each wave were accompanied by crashing sounds of anchor chains tossed about in steel-floored lockers, and crescendo whinings of propellers momentarily airborne, as massive waves lifted the stern from the sea.

I was in charge of a 5-person unit, whose job was to measure and report the meteorolgical and ice conditions encountered on our voyage to and from the Boothia Peninsular, an area in the Canadian Arctic about 2,000 miles north of Minneapolis. Measuring wind direction and speed in heavy seas while holding a portable-vaned anemometer with both hands, and standing on the ship's flying bridge attached to a stanchion by a safety cable, could be a tricky maneuver. Even more so, in the company of screeching wind, horizontal rain and blowing spume. At the extreme of listing to one side, there were times when I wondered if the ship might go belly up, but the next wall of the heaving sea always provided the lift and force to reverse the ship's leaning and send it healing in the opposite direction.

Getting from Seattle, Washington to the Arctic Ocean on an LST was slow business. Our progress each 24 hours was about 200 miles. A week before we reached the Arctic Ocean, a large band of ice became visible along the northern horizon. This was odd because I knew from aircraft reports that the nearest sea ice was many hundreds of miles further north. The band of ice had to be reasonably close, because from the deck of our LST the distance to the horizon was seven nautical miles.

Through binoculars the features of the ice suggested a wall, like the leading face of a glacier, but we were hundreds of miles from the nearest land. It wasn't an iceberg because they didn't occur in this part of the Northern Pacific Ocean. For three days we sailed directly towards the wall of ice, but it always kept its distance. On the fourth day it was gone.

What we had been looking at was a mirage, the first I'd ever seen at sea. They result from air temperature differences that cause the atmosphere to act as a mirror. The image on the horizon was of ice in the ocean hundreds of miles away. After the surprise encounter with a wall of ice far out in the ocean, and observing its mysterious behavior, it was easier to understand how mirage sightings by ancient seafarers sometimes spawned incredible stories.

When we reached the Arctic Ocean daylight was constantly present, its brightness diminishing as the sun dipped near, or temporarily below the horizon in the hours around midnight. For a short period during the summer, the edge of the Arctic ice pack moves offshore a short distance, creating a narrow, shallow channel close to the beach. With help from an icebreaker, our convoy of LST's successfully navigated the passage along the coasts of Alaska, Yukon, Northwest Territories and Nunavut, occasionally catching the attention of a polar bear who watched from an ice floe.

Except for views of the Brooks Range as we passed near Point Barrow, Alaska, the landscape we encountered along the entire Arctic coast of North America was endless tundra. Occasionally, we sighted 10 to 12 feet tall structures on the tundra made of several whale ribs bound together and standing upright like the poles inside of a tepee. Placed there by natives, these navigation aids function like destination signs on an interstate highway. Once while I was scanning the tundra, a whale surfaced next to the ship and I looked directly down into its blowhole, about ten feet away, unfortunately without a camera in hand.

Our LST carried thousands of barrels of fuel oil in the ship's hold and strapped two layers high on its open decks. The fuel would power the heavy equipment and generators used to construct an airfield and radar station on the tundra at our destination. The last hundred yards of our trip was an exciting, noisy, bumpy ride at full throttle headed directly to shore. LST's are designed to make beach landings whereupon their bow doors open and their cargo is offloaded. At a precise moment in the race towards the beach an anchor attached to a long cable is dropped from the ship's stern. When it comes time to back off the beach, a powerful wench rewinds the stern anchor cable, pulling the ship away from shore. About a week into unloading the oil drums onto the Boothia Peninsula, a group of Eskimos arrived on foot from across the tundra. We learned that these natives of Nunavat came to see the iron ships, because they had never before seen one. How they knew we were there remained a mystery. After a day, they walked out of sight back across the tundra.

Returning from the Arctic, with lots of leave time accumulated, I was ready for a break. I bought a Greyhound ticket and boarded the bus for New York City. After days of looking out the window at the plains of Montana and North Dakota, I had developed a terrible case of cabin fever. I left the bus in Chicago

ABOUT THE AUTHOR

RICHARD LYNCH was born and raised in Brooklyn, New York, not far from downtown, in what is now called Cobble Hill. He lived with his parents, two sisters, and three brothers. At first his world was quite small, centering around his home on Warren Street, the Roman Catholic parochial school half a block to the right of the house, and St. Paul's Church, around the corner to the left and down the block.

As he grew up, all of New York City opened up to him, thanks to public transportation and the more casual approaches to parenting that were prevalent at the time. He explored all about the city and soon expanded his adventures to include much of the upper half of the Eastern Seaboard.

After five years at Bishop Loughlin High School, knowing that he was about to be drafted, Richard joined the US Navy. He learned to be a weatherman which took him to Alaska, the Bering Sea, Washington State, San Diego, and finally, to Bikini Atoll in the Pacific Ocean. It was there, as an observer and weather forecaster for atomic and hydrogen bomb tests, that he became interested in science, initially because he admired the scientists, who seemed unencumbered by the strict rules and ranks of the armed service.

Richard had earned a high-school equivalency diploma while

in the Navy and decided that he would go to medical school. After being discharged from the service, he went home to Brooklyn, worked full time in an insurance company and attended Brooklyn College at night. Noting that an MD was very far away at that pace, he decided on a new approach, applying to state schools in the Midwest where he thought he could study full time and live on his GI Bill allotment. The University of Missouri accepted him first and he relocated to Columbia where he studied, worked in a lab, and got himself accepted at the University of Rochester School of Medicine.

Still interested in the scientific basis of medicine, Richard went on to train in Pathology at Washington University in St. Louis and joined the faculty there. In 1981, he came to the University of Iowa as Chair of the Pathology Department, a position he held until 2000. He was always involved in research and ran a large research lab with many technicians, students, fellows, and other trainees. In addition, he was the author of numerous scientific papers and participated in national and international committees and scientific organizations to benefit research and medical education.

While in Rochester, Richard met and married his wife Nancy. Together, they had three children; Alison, Brendan, and Matthew, and raised them all to be the kind of people you can be proud of.

Richard was simply the nicest, most decent person in the whole world. He died of cancer in 2009 and is still very much missed by his family and by many friends.